WALKING THE MUNROS

Volume One:
Southern, Central and Western Highlands

ABOUT THE AUTHOR

Steve Kew made his first solo climb at the age of 11 in the Lake District when he pioneered an interesting route from his campsite in Grasmere to the summit of Helm Crag; he has been hooked on mountains ever since. He attended a beginners' rock climbing course in 1970 and immediately returned to do the intermediate and advanced courses. Since then he has climbed and walked extensively throughout Britain; in the Alps he has done many of the classic 4000m peaks such as the Matterhorn, Nadelgrat and Monte Rosa traverse and has been on several trekking and climbing trips to the Nepal Himalayas and the Karakoram. He lives in southwest Scotland where he is a member of the Galloway Mountain Rescue Team and Chairman of the Stewartry Mountaineering Club. His previous writing includes three other books, many articles for newspapers and magazines and radio drama for the BBC. This is his first guidebook.

WALKING THE MUNROS

Volume One:
Southern, Central and Western Highlands

by
Steve Kew

2 POLICE SQUARE, MILNTHORPE, CUMBRIA LA7 7PY
www.cicerone.co.uk

A catalogue record for this book is available from the British Library.

ACKNOWLEDGEMENTS

I am grateful to the Ordnance Survey for permission to base my own maps and measurements on the OS 1:50,000 series, and to Lucy Histed and Hazel Clarke for helpful suggestions on creating the maps and organising the guide.

I am also indebted to Beathag Mhoireasan from the Gaelic College in Sleat – Sabhal Mòr Ostaig – for invaluable help with the Gaelic names and pronunciations. Any mistakes or oddities in the handling of these names in the text, however, is entirely my own fault.

Thanks also are due to Jean Etherington for helping to keep track of where I was on my travels, and also to the numerous youth hostel wardens and local police with whom I left details of routes.

I am also grateful to Ronald Turnbull for his suggestions on the text.

The short quote from *The Songs of Duncan Ban Macintyre* in the section on Beinn Dorain comes from a translation by Angus Macleod, published by Oliver and Boyd for the Scottish Gaelic Texts Society 1952. It is worth getting hold of this book, if only for an extraordinary description it contains of the qualities of the water in a little burn on the east side of Beinn Dorain called the Allt na h-Annait.

Above all this was for Tink, who was with me every step of the way.

Maps are based on Ordnance Survey ® material, licence number PU100012932.

ADVICE TO READERS

Readers are advised that while every effort is taken by the author to ensure the accuracy of this guidebook, changes can occur which may affect the contents. It is also advisable to check locally on transport, accommodation, shops, etc.

The author would welcome information on any updates and changes. Please send to the author care of Cicerone Press, 2 Police Square, Milnthorpe, Cumbria LA7 7PY

Front cover: Ben Alder across the Allt a'Chadil-reidhe

CONTENTS

Map Symbols

△	Munro summit
○	Munro Top
	Road
	Track
	Railway
	Route
	Alternative route
	Rivers
	Loch/sea

Contours:
For the sake of simplicity only four contours have been used. They are intended to indicate the general shape of the hills and to include prominent features such as summit ridges. Because the height of the Munros varies considerably (between 915m and 1344m) these contours may designate differing heights from map to map.

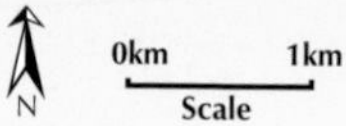

Okm 1km
Scale
N

Direction of grid (north) and scale in kilometres

Ⓟ

Parking

■

Buildings/habitation

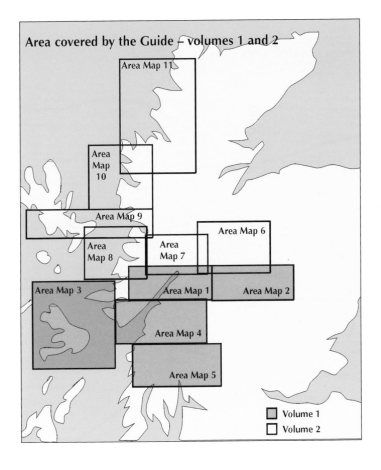

Area covered by the Guide – volumes 1 and 2

Area Map 11

Area Map 10

Area Map 9

Area Map 6

Area Map 8

Area Map 7

Area Map 3

Area Map 1

Area Map 2

Area Map 4

Area Map 5

Volume 1
Volume 2

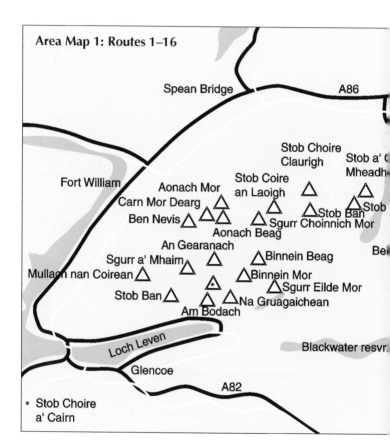

Area Map 1: Routes 1–16

Spean Bridge

A86

Stob Choire
Claurigh

Stob a' (
Mheadh

Fort William

Aonach Mor

Carn Mor Dearg

Ben Nevis

Stob Coire
an Laoigh

Stob

Stob Ban

Stob

Sgurr Choinnich Mor

Aonach Beag

An Gearanach

Sgurr a' Mhaim

Binnein Beag

Bei

Mullach nan Coirean

Binnein Mor

Sgurr Eilde Mor

Stob Ban

Na Gruagaichean

Am Bodach

Loch Leven

Blackwater resvr.

Glencoe

A82

* Stob Choire
   a' Cairn

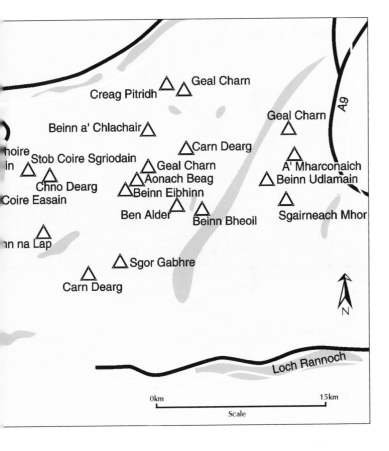

Creag Pitridh △ △ Geal Charn

Geal Charn △

Beinn a' Chlachair △

△Carn Dearg

hoire
in △ Stob Coire Sgriodain
△ Chno Dearg

△ Geal Charn
△Aonach Beag
△Beinn Eibhinn

A' Mharconaich
△ Beinn Udlamain

Coire Easain

Ben Alder △ △ Beinn Bheoil

△ Sgairneach Mhor

n na Lap △

△ Sgor Gabhre

△ Carn Dearg

N

0km   15km
Scale

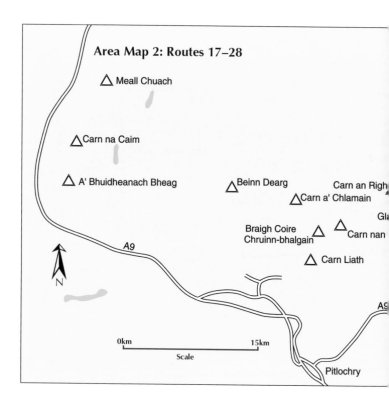

Area Map 2: Routes 17–28

△ Meall Chuach

△ Carn na Caim

△ A' Bhuidheanach Bheag

△ Beinn Dearg

Carn an Righ

△ Carn a' Chlamain

Gla

Braigh Coire
Chruinn-bhalgain △ △ Carn nan

N

A9

△ Carn Liath

A9

0km   15km

Scale

Pitlochry

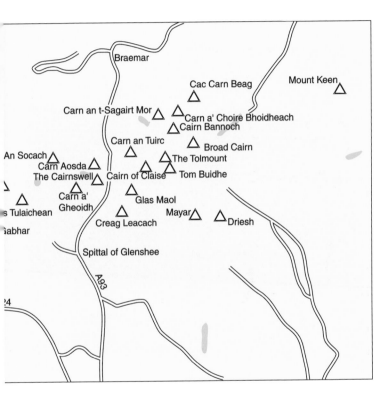

Patches of snow still lying on Aonach Beag in late August (Route 2)

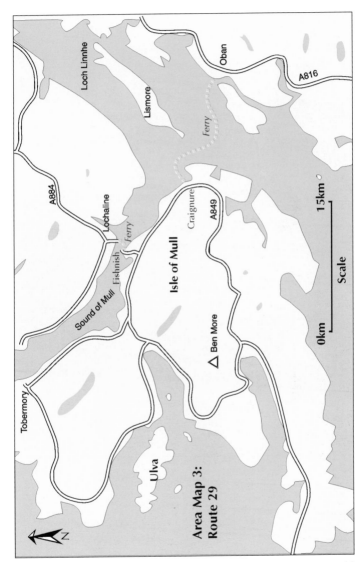

Area Map 3:
Route 29

15

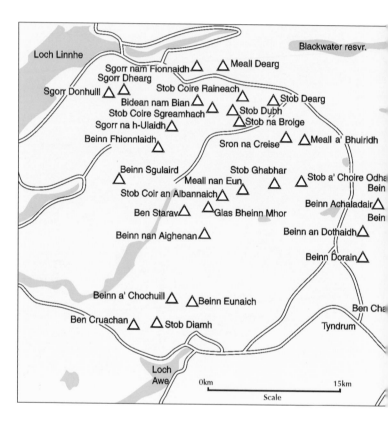

Loch Linnhe

Blackwater resvr.

Sgorr nam Fionnaidh △   △ Meall Dearg
Sgorr Dhearg
Sgorr Donhuill △ △
Stob Coire Raineach
Sgorr Donhuill △ △   △ Stob Dearg
          Bidean nam Bian △ △
Stob Coire Sgreamhach   △ Stob Dubh
Sgorr na h-Ulaidh △   △ Stob na Broige
Beinn Fhionnlaidh   Sron na Creise △   △ Meall a' Bhuiridh
          △
                        Stob Ghabhar
    Beinn Sgulaird   △ Stob a' Choire Odha
          Meall nan Eun   Bein
    △   Stob Coir an Albannaich △   △
Stob Coir an Albannaich   Beinn Achaladair △
    Ben Starav △ △ Glas Bheinn Mhor   Bein
                              Beinn an Dothaidh △
Beinn nan Aighenan △
                              Beinn Dorain △

    Beinn a' Chochuill △ △ Beinn Eunaich
                                        Ben Cha
Ben Cruachan △ △ Stob Diamh   Tyndrum

Loch
Awe   0km   15km
                   Scale

16

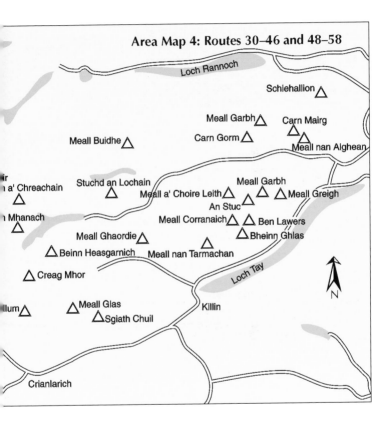

Area Map 4: Routes 30–46 and 48–58

Loch Rannoch

Schiehallion △

Meall Garbh △   Carn Mairg △ △
Carn Gorm △   Meall nan Aighean △

Meall Buidhe △

r
a' Chreachain   Stuchd an Lochain   Meall Garbh
△   △   Meall a' Choire Leith △ △ △ Meall Greigh
                                    An Stuc
Mhanach   Meall Corranaich △ △ Ben Lawers
△   △ Bheinn Ghlas
              Meall Ghaordie △
           △ Beinn Heasgarnich   Meall nan Tarmachan
                                        △
        △ Creag Mhor   Loch Tay

                                                N

llum △   △ Meall Glas
           △ Sgiath Chuil   Killin

    Crianlarich

17

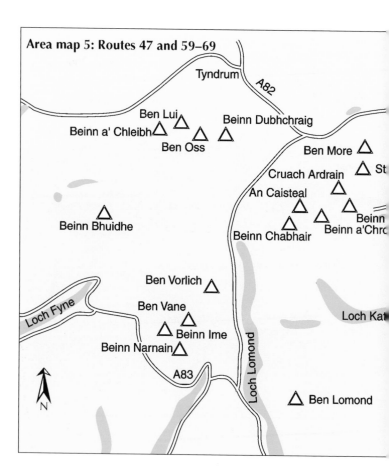

Area map 5: Routes 47 and 59–69

Tyndrum A82

Ben Lui
Beinn a' Chleibh
Ben Oss
Beinn Dubhchraig

Ben More
Cruach Ardrain St
An Caisteal
Beinn Bhuidhe
Beinn Chabhair
Beinn a'Chro
Beinn

Ben Vorlich

Loch Fyne
Ben Vane
Beinn Ime
Beinn Narnain
A83

Loch Lomond

Loch Kat

Ben Lomond

N

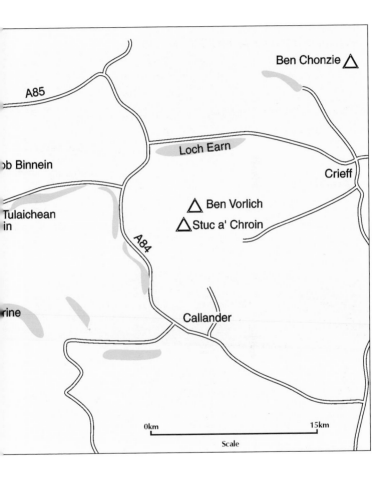

Aonach Eagach from Glen Coe (Route 31)

INTRODUCTION

There are 284 Munros – that's a lot of cheese sandwiches. It's a lot of blisters, too, and sweat and tired muscles and wet socks. But think of the positive side. Doing the Munros will take you to places of quite extraordinary beauty that you would never otherwise have seen; places that inspire awe, reflection and sometimes fear. The pleasures awaiting the Munroist are many and varied. Navigating your way through the primeval wonderland of Scotland's mountain landscapes will put the rest of your life into a new perspective. There will be moments of great satisfaction, often in the midst of adversity; moments when you have unforgettable encounters with wildlife, and moments when friendships are forged through shared experience.

Climbing the Munros can also give you a richer understanding of the forces that have shaped this great landscape, and an appreciation of the lives of those hardy creatures and plants that depend upon it for their existence. It will perhaps introduce you to some of the great stories of Scottish history that have been played out in the Highlands. If you are lucky it might even give you a greater understanding of your own inner strengths and weaknesses, a discovery of where your own limits lie and a chance to stretch yourself beyond them. There is a lot to be gained from walking the Scottish hills.

Rainbow on the Aonachs from Sgurr Choinnich Beag (Route 2)

Ben Alder from the northeast ridge (Route 14)

So why is there a need for this new guide to the Munros when there are other more lavishly illustrated guides on the market? The answer became clear to me when I saw walkers carrying scribbled route descriptions and crumpled photocopies with them on walks. Big, hardback guidebooks are fine for a coffee table, but they can't be slipped into your back pocket and taken with you where they're really needed. This guide, with its waterproof jacket, can be taken on your walk, and gives a full, clear and up-to-date route description.

Let's be honest about it: doing the Munros is not as hard as it once was. The logistics are much easier now, for a start; within the lifetime of one generation many of the Highland roads have become wider, straighter and faster. Where once you had to wait until morning for a ferryman to arrive and take one or two cars across at a time, now there is a bridge. There are also more people walking the hills; routes are well established and danger points better understood. A good safety net is also provided by mountain rescue teams across the country in the event of things going wrong. Route-finding is also much easier than it used to be, with a network of paths on most of the major hills where thousands of others have gone before. But – and it is a big but – climbing the Munros is still an adventure; one that will grip you and give you a fund of memories to last a lifetime. And when the weather turns bad there is just the same need as ever there was for sound judgement, fortitude and navigational skill to bring you safely home.

The qualities required of the Munroist are not technically or even physically as demanding as those, say, of the rock climber or the high-altitude mountaineer (unless the routes are being done in winter conditions, in which case they can become a serious and arduous mountaineering under-taking). But a certain doggedness is nevertheless needed – the perseverance to see through a huge task – plus the skill and courage to navigate in conditions that can change all too rapidly in the Scottish hills. And this is not to mention a willingness to get wet, cold, shrouded in mist and buffeted by storms. If you only venture out when the sun is shining on the tops it may take more than one lifetime to complete the round.

Some people may deride those who are working through the Munros, as if the act of ticking them off a list somehow corrupts an otherwise pure experience of mountaineering. In my experience the opposite is true. By accepting the challenge of doing them all you open yourself up to a host of new experiences, and you find yourself in a variety of mountain situations that you might never have otherwise experienced. Besides this, of the many accomplished and aspiring Munroists I know, I can think of none who confine their hillwalking just to the peaks that are on the list. I know of none who have not felt enriched by trying to complete the round.

Stob Corie nam Beith from Glen Coe (Route 32)

THE MUNROS

What exactly are the Munros? I don't propose here to retell the history of this select group of hills. Suffice to say that Sir Hugh Munro's great idea of climbing all the 3000ft mountains in Scotland has for over a century captured the imagination of everyone who loves mountains. In the popular imagination the Round of Munros includes all the hills that are over 3000ft in height. Once you start climbing them, however, you quickly realize that this is not the whole story. There are many points where the land rises above 3000ft but is not regarded as a separate hill; or where it clearly is a separate hill, but it has still not been accorded the status of a Munro.

Sir Hugh's original list, drawn up in 1891, was rather different from the most recently updated version. Some

revisions have taken place as a result of improvements in mapping. Sir Hugh, for example, rather conveniently believed that the Inaccessible Pinnacle was lower than Sgurr Dearg and so it was not originally listed as a Munro. Even today the latest satellite mapping techniques may reveal that the accepted heights of hills is wrong (usually only by the odd metre). The Munro summit of Ben a' Chroin had to be redefined a couple of years ago because what was previously thought to be a lower Top nearly 1km away was found to be 1m higher than the classified summit. Similarly the respective heights of Beinn a' Chaorainn's three summits have recently been revised, and Ben Nevis itself is now officially 1m lower than it was a few years ago.

Successive revisions of the list by the Great and the Good have sought to declassify some hills and upgrade others, not just because their respective heights have been reassessed but also on the basis of their 'character' or 'remoteness', or whether it was felt that readers ought to be directed to one rather than another. There is not always an obvious logic to the hills that are in or out of the list at any moment in time, and the list has been revised so often that it is in some danger of being discredited. The last revision came in 1997, and on the current list there are 284 Munros and 227 Tops.

Despite all the argument and lack of clarity about what makes a hill a Munro, and despite the all-too-frequent revisions, there is no doubting the fact that the underlying idea of the list makes sense to most people; it always has made sense and it probably always will. The list stands for something meaningful both to the hillwalker and to the public at large, and that something involves the idea that the Munros are all the highest hills in Scotland.

USING THE GUIDE

This guide is published in two volumes: volume one covering the southern Munros and volume two the northern peaks. In general the routes in volume one are listed from west to east and from north to south. Ben Nevis and Carn Mor Dearg, in the far northwest of the area covered by this volume, therefore make up Route 1, followed by the Munros that extend eastwards along the Spean Valley. The Arrochar Alps and

Ben Lomond, being the most southerly Munros, are listed last.

The routes described are often the most popular ones for each hill; usually these are also the most direct and obvious ways up. Like most walkers I have a preference for circuits rather than returning by the route of ascent, and these have been given where appropriate. Some alternatives to the described route are indicated. There may be 'better' ways up some of the hills, but the distances involved in reaching them can be a strong disincentive to their use.

Some Munros are isolated and have to be climbed on their own, but most Munros fall naturally into distinct pairs or small groups. Sometimes,

Near the top of the Lancet Edge on Sgor Iutharn (Geal Charn) (Route 15)

however, this natural grouping of hills can make for a very long route if done in one outing. Usually these longer routes, such as the Lochnagar circuit or the Ben Lui hills, can be broken down into shorter walks if required, and whilst several long routes are described here in full, suggestions are made (where appropriate) about how to tackle them in a number of shorter outings if preferred.

Each route is prefaced by a box containing information to help you in planning your ascents.

MOUNTAIN NAMES AND PRONUNCIATIONS

All the mountain names have been taken in the form that they appear on the current 1:50,000 OS maps, although it is clear that there could be alternative spellings for many of them. Spellings on the maps sometimes appear in their Gaelic form, for example 'bheinn' and 'mhor', and sometimes in anglicized versions of Gaelic words, such as 'ben' and 'more'. For the sake of consistency I have kept faithful to the OS spellings, even where these appear to be wrong.

Suggested meanings and pronunciations have been given at the start of each route for the names of all the peaks, drawing on a variety of sources. The origin of mountain names is often complex and sometimes obscure. Whilst the majority of Scottish mountain names are of Gaelic origin, some owe more to Norse, Pictish, Scots or English influence. Some names may contain elements of more than one language – Bla Bheinn on Skye, for example, is often held to derive from 'bla', a Norse word meaning 'blue', and 'bheinn', the Gaelic word for mountain, although there are others who feel that Bla comes from the Gaelic 'blath', meaning 'flowers'. Many Munro names have more than one possible derivation.

Pronunciations, too, are far from fixed and certain, and it would be wrong to be too dogmatic about them. I have tried to give a simple phonetic rendition of each pronunciation so that a modern English speaker can readily understand it. But this is not a simple task: many of the names may have Gaelic roots, but over time they have been corrupted into words that are no longer recognisably Gaelic. Ben Chonzie, for example, may have its origin in the Gaelic word 'còineach', meaning moss, but there is no letter z in the Gaelic alphabet, and the name as it appears on maps today is no more recognisable to a Gaelic speaker than it is to an English speaker.

Putting these names into phonetic spellings presents other difficulties too. Gaelic has a number of sounds which have no equivalent in English, for example the Gaelic sound 'ch' (as in the word 'loch') is always a soft sound produced in the back of the throat, not the harder English sound of 'lock' or the 'ch' sound produced in the front of the mouth (as in 'chalk').

Aonach Dubh from the lip of the upper Corrie of Coire nan Lochan (Route 32)

Moreover Gaelic has distinct regional differences in pronunciation, and in some areas where Gaelic is no longer spoken the local pronunciations of mountain names may not accord with received wisdom about the 'correct' pronunciation.

Many people regard it as a form of vandalism to change old names in any way, and whilst I have a lot of sympathy with this view I am also aware that language can never be frozen in time. The historical evidence shows clearly that, like other place names, the names of Munros have changed and evolved over time. There is nothing inherently wrong with modern usage bringing new changes to these words. There is no one period in history to which the 'correct' pronunciation should be attributed.

MAPS

The maps accompanying each route are based on the 2002 editions of the Ordnance Survey 1:50,000 series maps. With the notable exception of one or two areas, such as the Black Cuillin on Skye, this is the scale of map that I personally prefer for climbing the Munros, and it is widely recognized as being a suitable scale of map for the hillwalker. The box at the start of each walk also makes reference to the relevant OS Explorer maps, which some people might prefer. These 1:25,000 maps give much more detail, which can be advantageous at times, but it can also complicate the process of routefinding – particularly on steep ground where a lot of contours are packed very close together, or in areas where there is a lot of exposed rock.

Sometimes more than one map is needed to cover the walk in question. Munros are listed on the covers of the Explorer maps in which they appear, but unfortunately some of these lists are currently inaccurate. Some hills that are not officially Munros have been accorded Munro status; others that are Munros have not been listed. No doubt this will be rectified in future editions of these maps.

The 'area maps' referred to in the box at the start of each route correspond to those at the start of the book; these are designed to give a broad view of where each Munro lies in relation to major roads and also to neighbouring Munros. The overview map of Scotland accompanying these area maps shows the location of each area within Scotland as a whole.

Glas Bheinn Mhor from Stob Corie Dheirg (Route 38)

The sketch maps accompanying each route description are designed to assist in planning route-finding. Although they are drawn to scale based on the OS 1:50,000 series maps, they are not intended to be a replacement for the OS maps for the purposes of navigation, and it is strongly recommended that the appropriate OS map is carried at all times. Harvey also make an excellent series of maps for some of the areas described.

If you are using different maps, or an older edition of the OS maps, you should bear in mind that spot heights and names may vary from those in the text.

GRID REFERENCES

As an aid to navigation, grid references have been given for summits and for other key features and descent points on all the routes. These are all 10-figure readings taken on the walk itself with a GPS. Whilst GPS readings can sometimes be inaccurate by 50m or more, they are usually much more accurate than this and are nearly always close enough for hillwalking purposes. (In a number of recent mountain rescue exercises small canes were planted in rough ground in a mountain area of several square miles and were found without much difficulty from their grid reference using a GPS, even in poor visibility.) The next generation of GPSs is likely to be even more accurate and reliable. Many walkers now carry a GPS and it can be a useful navigational

Brocken spectre on the ridge between Creise and Meall a' Bhuiridh (Route 40)

tool, especially if you need to establish your exact position in poor visibility. This does not obviate the need for a map and compass, however, and great care needs to be taken if you are navigating from one waypoint to another in poor visibility, as a straight line between the two may well take you over a cliff.

DISTANCE AND ASCENT

The distances given in the information box at the start of each walk are always from the car park and back to the car park unless otherwise stated. The ascent for each route includes the cumulative height gained over undulating ground.

DIFFICULTY

Climbing any Munro involves a degree of difficulty. A fair level of fitness, an ability to navigate using a map and compass in poor visibility and an understanding of the mountain environment are all necessary qualities for anyone attempting to climb a Munro, and it is assumed that anyone using this guide will have these minimum skills.

In certain walks, additional skills are required for activities such as scrambling on rock, dealing with exposure or crossing rivers. Notes on 'difficulty' appear in the preface to such walks. However, the absence of any mention of specific problems does not imply that a walk is necessarily 'easy' or to be taken lightly. The usual grading system for scrambling has been used, that is from grade 1 for relatively simple scrambles to grade 3 for relatively hard ones.

There are certain ranges of Scottish mountains that pose special difficulties

The following books may be useful for developing mountain skills:

- Terry Adby and Stuart Johnston, *The Hillwalker's Guide to Mountaineering* (Cicerone Press, 2003)

- Eric Langmuir, *Mountaincraft and Leadership* (Scottish Sports Council – SportScotland, 1995).

The rocks of Stob Corie Dhorie looking towards Ghlas Bheinn Mhor (Route 38)

or dangers for the walker or climber and I have written special introductions for the Munros on the Isle of Skye, and for those in the Cairngorms, to highlight these dangers. These area observations (which both occur in Volume 2) precede the relevant routes and should be read before attempting any of the walks in these areas.

take too long. Above all, every effort has been made to be consistent so that each walker can get used to the values given in relation to their own speed. Bear in mind that the times given do not include elements for stoppages, lunch breaks, etc, which should be added on.

TIMES

Approximate route times are given in the information box for each route. These have been worked out using an adapted version of Naismith's rule, combined with common sense and my own experience of the character of the route. Some walkers will consistently achieve faster times; others will be slower. It really doesn't matter which, except on very long routes where you may run the risk of benightment if you

PARKING AND STARTING THE WALK

Details are given in the walk information box about the best places to park for each walk and how to access the hill from these points. It should be borne in mind, however, that approved places for parking are more liable to change than other aspects of a route, and you should be prepared for possible local changes. In a similar vein getting from the road onto the hill frequently takes walkers through a fringe of forest or through farms or other habitation where the preferred line of access may change from time to time. Please ensure that you follow local signs.

ACCOMMODATION AND CAMPSITES

The nearest youth hostel is given in the information box and, where appropriate, the nearest Independent Hostel. It should be noted, however, that there are some routes, for example in Glen Clova and Glen Esk, where the nearest hostel is a very considerable distance away. For most routes the box also gives the nearest centre where hotels or bed and breakfast accommodation can be found. Occasionally a specific hotel is named if it is the only accommodation in the immediate vicinity of the route.

An indication of where the nearest campsites are has also been given for each route. Unfortunately campsites seem to come and go with some rapidity. 'Wild camping' is generally accepted in remote areas well away from the road, so long as the usual rules about rubbish and waste disposal are observed; but the practice of roadside camping – which is currently widespread – is strongly frowned on by landowners, local councils, the police and others.

ACCESS

The Land Reform Act (Scotland), which was passed by the Scottish parliament in 2003, greatly clarifies the issue of access to Scottish mountains, most of which are privately owned. Whilst it bestows a general right of access to the walker, it does not change the need for

Beinn a' Chreachain (in cloud) from Beinn Achaladair (Route 42)

considerate behaviour in terms of closing gates, protecting stone dykes, taking home litter and respecting both the livestock and wildlife that live in the hills. Nor does it change the need to avoid conflict with other users. In fact, these responsibilities have been built into the bill in the form of a Code of Access, along with the requirement that walkers shoulder responsibility for their own safety. Details can currently be viewed on www.snh.org.uk.

There are critical times in the life of upland estates when particular care should be taken. These include the lambing season from March to early summer, and the stalking season – which for stags is from July to October (the latter part of this period is the most critical time for many estates) and for hinds is from late October to mid-February. The shooting season for grouse runs from 12th August to mid-December.

Certain estates in the recent past have not welcomed walkers at all, particularly during the stalking season, and there have been one or two well-publicized battles over access. Fortunately the vast majority of estates now have an enlightened view about public access and many subscribe to the hillphones scheme (see box) or put up notices and maps at the start of walks to assist walkers. Some estates have even constructed car parks specifically for the use of hillwalkers. Dogs can be a serious nuisance. The Access Code gives clear guidelines on keeping dogs under proper control.

Hillphones scheme

This scheme provides hillwalkers in a number of areas in upland Scotland with daily information about deer-stalking activities. Recorded messages indicate where stalking is taking place and which walking routes will be unlikely to affect stalking, and give a forecast of stalking activity over the next few days. The messages are generally updated by 8am each day and are charged at normal call rates. Walks in areas covered by the scheme have the hillphones number in the 'Access' section of the box at the start of each route. For further information contact www.hill-phones.info

Whilst many estates like walkers to ring the factor's office or head stalker to discuss their routes before venturing onto the hill during the stag-stalking season, most are happy for walkers to come even at this time of year, providing they don't interfere with stalking. Generally speaking, walkers would be advised to keep to ridges and high ground rather than to move through corries when stalking is taking place. There is less likely to be a conflict at weekends than midweek. On Sundays no shooting at all takes place. If in any doubt try ringing the relevant contact number for advice, but bear in mind that estate offices are not always manned throughout the day.

Beinn Mhanach (centre) (Route 43)

Co-operation isn't always straight-forward: stalkers – the gillies – often don't know in which area they will be working until the morning of the day in question, and contacting them at that time may not be possible. There should rarely be access problems for most of the routes described provided you act responsibly and try to avoid conflict with other countryside users. Every effort has been made in this guide to give up-to-date contacts for every walk (see 'Access' in the box at the start of each walk), but it should be remembered that, just like other sorts of property, estates do sometimes change hands. For smaller estates where the contact may be a stalker's home number, both the person and the phone number can change fairly often.

A number of routes are accessed by crossing railway lines, and at the time of writing Network Rail are proposing to close some 600 unattended railway crossings to the public on the grounds of safety. There have occasionally been accidents involving walkers crossing railway lines, and walkers should make sure that they cross only at designated places or have the necessary permission to cross from Network Rail. Future Munroists should be aware that new legislation in this area might necessitate changes to the start of some walks.

PATHS

The passage of many feet has left paths on most of the popular routes, and in some places on the lower slopes these paths are robustly constructed. Many walkers may prefer not to travel on such paths, but it should be remembered that constructed paths are there to prevent unnecessary erosion in a fragile landscape. They also limit the disturbance to nesting birds and other wildlife. In some of the walks in this guide you are strongly urged to keep to the described route; this may be because of the particular vulnerability of certain landscapes or to avoid conflict with other land users such as stalkers and shooters at particular times of the year. Path repair and management projects are not there to make the walking easier but to protect the quality of the mountain landscape and its ecology. On the other side of the coin, the Munroist should never assume that there will be a path – particularly on the higher slopes – or that, if there is, it can easily be followed. Anyone who has such an expectation will be quickly disillusioned.

Throughout the guide a distinction is drawn between roads, tracks and paths. 'Road' is used to indicate a tarmacked public road. 'Track' is used to denote a forestry road or a private estate road or landrover track where the public does not have a right of vehicular access and where the road surface is usually rough (sometimes very rough), but where a bike could perhaps be used. 'Path' is used to denote a constructed footpath, or one that has formed over time by the passage of many feet. Bikes should not be taken on these. Some paths are startlingly obvious features cutting brashly across the countryside; others may be almost non-existent.

Beinn Narnain from Beinn Ime (Route 68)

BIKES

The use of mountain bikes by hillwalkers on estate roads has become very widespread in the Highlands. There are hills which lie so far from any public road that the use of a bike to approach the hill along a forestry track or estate road can save many hours of walking. Opinion is split on whether or not this is a good thing. Some people prefer the long walk in. The National Trust has been trying to encourage a pedestrian approach: in some cases – for example in the Mar Lodge Estate in the Cairngorms – by digging up some of the estate roads and turning them back into footpaths.

My own view is that the wilderness character of remote areas needs to be strenuously protected from vehicular access and other sorts of development. There seems to be little restraint even today on the creation of new private roads in Scotland's fragile wilderness areas; but as long as there is a road leading to the hill, used by estate workers and their clients in their heavy four-by-fours, I can see no valid reason why a bike should not be used on it too. Whatever one's position on this, there is widespread agreement that mountain bikes should not be taken beyond these tracks onto footpaths.

LEAVING WORD

Walkers should always leave word with someone about their intended route and expected time of return. Youth hostels throughout the Highlands have specially printed route cards. These can be filled in and left with the hostel in case you have an accident. Police stations throughout the area have similar forms, and in hillwalking areas the police are usually very helpful to walkers. They are, after all, the first point of contact if a mountain rescue team has to be called out. In preparing this book I did all the Munros solo and frequently left details of where I was going at local police stations.

Bear in mind, though, that many of the smaller police stations in the Highlands – even in major climbing centres like Braemar – are not manned every day. Always speak to an officer just to be sure, otherwise the scribbled note you put through the letterbox describing your proposed route may not be picked up for several days. It may be better to contact one of the larger regional stations such as Fort William or Inverness. These are always manned and many of the staff will be knowledgeable about routes and well versed in rescue procedures should the need arise. It is of course essential that if you leave a route card with someone, you must return or ring them up to let them know you have got back safely. Mountain rescuers never mind going onto the hill to search for someone in trouble, but they do not take kindly to searching for someone who has gone home and forgotten, or simply not bothered, to tell anyone that they got back. The time and effort that go into such searches is often considerable.

In the event of an emergency, contact the local police or ring 999 and be prepared to say where the emergency has arisen, with a grid reference if at all possible. If you are carrying a mobile phone bear in mind that in large parts of the Highlands it is not possible to get a signal. Your best chance of getting a signal in many mountain areas may be high up on the summits, but even here it may not be possible.

WHEN TO GO

This guide has been written with the summer walker in mind. Summer conditions will usually prevail between May and September, although deep-lying snow can last into the summer in some high places, affecting the safety

Beinn Narnain summit rocks from southeast approach (Route 68)

of otherwise 'easy' routes. 'Winter' storms are not uncommon in May or September – I have been caught out by snow in June! You should always obtain an up-to-date weather forecast from one of the many specialized forecast services before venturing into the Scottish hills. Avalanche warnings for specific areas are available on the internet at: www.sais.gov.uk.

In winter conditions many routes may not be possible without strong all-round mountaineering experience. Navigation becomes more difficult,

simple scrambles can become technical climbs, daylight is short and deteriorating weather can quickly lead to arctic conditions. Whilst a covering of snow can greatly add to the beauty and atmosphere of these mountains, remember that paths, cairns and other markers can quickly be obliterated; corniced ridges, snowdrifts and iced-up rock can make simple summer routes slow and fraught with danger. The Scottish hills should never be underestimated.

Enjoy them safely. Happy climbing!

NEVIS

ROUTE 1

Ben Nevis (1343m),
Carn Mor Dearg (1220m)

Pronunciation: *Ben Nevis; Karn More Jerrack*
Translation: *Venomous Mountain; Big Red Cairn*

Distance:	15km
Ascent:	1700m
Time:	7hrs
Difficulty:	Demanding route with exposed section (the Carn Mor Dearg arête) that in summer involves some simple scrambling (up to grade 1). Accurate navigation from summit of Ben Nevis is essential in poor weather.
Maps:	OS sheet 41; Explorer map 392; Harvey's Superwalker map Ben Nevis; Area Map 1
Parking:	Visitor centre car park or by YHA or at Ben Nevis Inn
Start:	footpath from Glen Nevis, which is stepped and engineered
Hostel:	YHA Glen Nevis; Independent Glen Nevis
B&B/hotel:	Fort William
Camping:	Glen Nevis
Access:	Bidwells, tel: 01397 702433; John Muir Trust, tel: 0131 554 0114

This tough, long route takes you on a spectacular circuit around the Nevis horseshoe to reach the highest point in Britain. It takes you through a wonderful variety of mountain terrain and includes some easy scrambling on the exposed Carn Mor Dearg arête. It is not the easiest way up Ben Nevis, however, and in poor weather can become a serious and demanding expedition.

To paraphrase Dickens: it is the best of hills, it is the worst of hills. The magnificent mountain architecture on the north side of Ben Nevis (or just 'the Ben' as it is affectionately known) offers one of the most awesome and impressive vistas in Britain – a huge and complex cathedral of rock, born of volcanic forces and massive intrusions of granite, relentless weathering and the scouring action of glaciation. It is a place that inspires fear and poetry and excitement. It is a magnet to everyone who loves mountains. But there is also the other Ben Nevis. A climber's first experience of reaching the summit on a clear summer's day is likely to come as a severe shock. There are often more people to be found here on a Saturday afternoon than in Sauchiehall Street, many of them totally ill-equipped and unprepared for a day on a mountain. The usual route from Glen Nevis is now like a motorway cut into the hill. The plateau itself is littered with cairns and frequently covered with litter. This is, apparently, the price of being the highest.

Despite all of this, the traverse described here is a wonderful route. Winter is definitely the best time to do it, when the tourist hordes are snuggled up at home in front of their fires, though in winter conditions it becomes a much more serious expedition which calls for all-round mountaineering skills.

Start from the visitor centre car park (12299 73088), from the YHA or from the Ben Nevis Inn (12591 72969). The paths from all three join not far up the hill. When the path begins to level out above Lochan Meall an t-Suidhe take a left fork. This eventually winds around to reach the CIC (Charles Inglis Clark) hut beneath the north face, but after about 1km leave this path and drop quite steeply down heather slopes to the Allt a' Mhuilinn. This can be crossed without difficulty at 15497 73792. This point can also be reached by a path from Torlundy, which has the advantage of shortening your encounter with the tourists. (If you prefer to approach the hill from this side, start from the North Face Car Park, which is signposted from the A82 in Torlundy. Don't try to access the Allt a' Mhuilinn via the golf course, as your presence will not be appreciated.)

From the river crossing, climb straight up the heathery hillside to Carn Beag Dearg. The slope soon

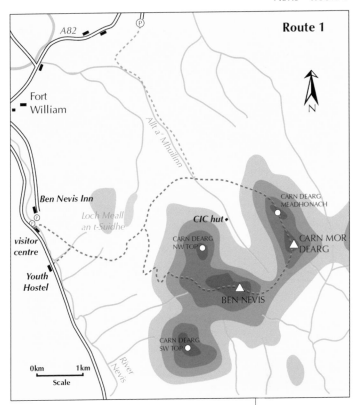

becomes bouldery. Stay on the crest of the ridge all the way to Carn Dearg Meadhonach (17602 72672). There is a lower path that traverses the west side of these hills to emerge below Carn Mor Dearg, but the best views are to be had higher up – not only of the magnificent north face of Ben Nevis, but also of the dozens of gullies etched into the flanks of Aonach Mor across the valley to the east. From the summit of Carn Dearg Meadhonach drop down over the pink/grey granite boulders and then climb again to the summit of **Carn Mor Dearg** at 17753 72161 (4hrs 20mins from the YHA).

From here you drop down to the south with quite a substantial loss of height before the ridge eventually curves round to the southwest. Stay on or very close to the crest of the arête (which is little more than a line of piled-up blocks). It is narrow but not difficult or intimidating in summer weather. Soon the ascent begins, past an abseil post, which marks a possible line of descent into Coire Leis. Then comes a steep climb over large andesite boulders to the summit of **Ben Nevis** at 16687 71275. There is an intermittent path and a line of rusting posts which in very poor weather may be a useful guide to the top (5hrs 20mins).

Follow the tourist trail back to the valley. It is essential in poor visibility to find the right line of descent. There have been many fatalities where parties have either stumbled over the northeast face or mistaken one of the Glen Nevis gullies for the way off. If in any doubt walk 150m from the summit trig pillar on a grid bearing of 231°, then follow a second grid bearing of 282° for just over 1km to reach the top of the zigzags and safer ground. Don't forget to add the necessary adjustment for magnetic variation to these grid bearings. In 2006 the variation was just under 3°W. Follow the Mountain Trail down through the zigzags to rejoin the outward route.

Ben Nevis from Carn Mor Dearg arête

THE AONACHS

ROUTE 2

Aonach Mor (1221m), Aonach Beag (1234m)

Pronunciation: Ernoch More; Ernoch Bake
Translation: Big Ridge; Little Ridge

Distance:	15km
Ascent:	1240m
Time:	7hrs
Difficulty:	accurate navigation is essential, and in poor visibility can be notoriously difficult on these hills
Maps:	OS sheet 41; Explorer map 392; Harvey's Superwalker map Ben Nevis; Area Map 1
Parking:	car park at the end of Glen Nevis
Start:	footpath from the east end of the car park through Nevis gorge
Hostel:	YHA, Glen Nevis; Independent Glen Nevis
B&B/hotel:	Fort William
Camping:	Glen Nevis
Access:	Bidwells, tel: 01397 702433

These two grand old men of the Scottish hills have been somewhat humbled by the ski-lift developments on the northern flanks of Aonach Mor, but approached from Glen Nevis they have lost none of their rugged appeal. There is an air of seriousness about them. Like many grand old men they need to be approached with care.

Starting from Glen Nevis, follow the popular walk through the gorge, past the beautiful Steall waterfall, to the little wooden bridge over the Allt Coire Giubhsachan.

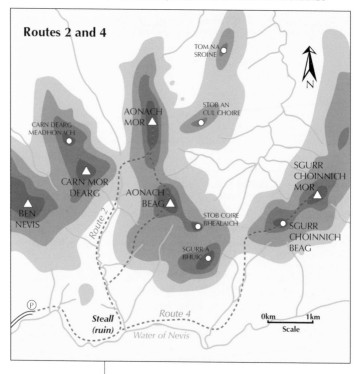

Aonach Mor is a granite mountain, being part of the Outer Granite of Ben Nevis. Aonach Beag is mostly composed of Dalradian schists. There has been extensive geological folding hereabouts. Impressive crags on both the east and west sides of these hills, which have been eroded into a series of deep gullies and scree slopes, limit the lines of escape in bad weather and add to the 'big mountain' feel of these tops. The huge bulk of the Ben Nevis horseshoe fills the western horizon.

Turn north just before the bridge and climb steeply alongside the burn with its attractive waterfalls to reach a huge open corrie. One side of this great amphitheatre is hemmed in by the southeastern edge of the Ben Nevis/Carn Mor Dearg horseshoe, whilst on the other side looms the great bulk of Aonach Mor and the craggy southwest ridge of Aonach Beag. Follow the path to the head of the corrie, where it climbs to a small col between Carn Mor Dearg and Aonach Mor 18715 72078 (2hrs 40mins).

Head east up a steep spur to arrive on easier ground at the southern end of Aonach Mor's broad plateau, then head north up the gentle incline of the plateau to **Aonach Mor**'s summit cairn at 19310 72942 (3hrs 50mins). There is little difficulty in finding the right line onto the plateau in ascent, but (for anyone using this as an escape route) finding the right descent line in poor visibility is not nearly so easy. An error in navigation could lead to dangerous ground if you try to descend either too far to the north or too far to the south. Start the descent at 19243 72210 and keep a close eye on the aspect of slope to make sure you aren't being lured off the right line.

From the summit of Aonach Mor, head south along the plateau, then south-southeast to cross the col between the two Aonachs. A glimpse over the edge to the

Glen Nevis

Aonach Beag from Sgurr Choinnich Mor

east here will often reveal patches of snow that have stayed in the shelter of these gullies right through the summer. There is some wonderful mountain scenery to admire on both sides. Climb the stony ridge to the summit of Aonach Beag, which despite its name is actually the bigger of the two hills. The cairn is some way back at 19713 71487 (4hrs 50mins).

The summit of **Aonach Beag** is dome shaped, and the whereabouts of the southwest ridge is not immediately clear from the top. Trusting your compass bearing, however, will soon bring the ridge into view. A path leads down, occasionally dodging round obstacles and always staying well to the left (east) of the main cliffs. It returns, steeply at times but without difficulty, past the old ruin to the little wooden bridge at Steall. From here it is plain sailing along the tourist path back to the car park.

THE GREY CORRIES

ROUTE 3

Stob Ban (977m), Stob Choire Claurigh (1177m), Stob Coire an Laoigh (1116m)

Pronunciation: Stob Ban;
Stob Horrer Clowree; Stob Korrer an Lui
Translation: White Peak; Peak of the
Clamouring Corrie; Peak of the Corrie of the Calf

Distance:	21km
Ascent:	1420m
Time:	7hrs 30mins
Difficulty:	river crossing must be made just above the dam to the north of Beinn na Socaich
Maps:	OS sheet 41; Explorer map 392; Harvey's Superwalker map Ben Nevis; Area Map 1
Parking:	by the old tramway (at 27019 72989) south of Corriechoille Farm. This is a private track, and whilst no objection is made at present to parking here, it would be well to check that this is acceptable in future.
Start:	continue south along private track
Hostel:	Independent Hostels at Inverroy and Tulloch
B&B/hotel:	Spean Bridge
Camping:	Inverroy; Roy Bridge
Access:	Bidwells, tel: 01397 702433

To the east of the Aonachs a fine group of hills called the Grey Corries stretch out across the Killiechonate Forest above Glen Spean. The Grey Corries offer excellent ridge walking with some good views across the central Highlands.

The point where the old tramway crosses the track is not obvious at first, but leave cars at GR 27019 78989 and continue along the gated track through the spruce forest into the well-defined pass, the Lairig Leacach. The track crosses to the east side of the Allt Leachdach for about 3km, then crosses back again towards the top of the pass before arriving after another 1.5km at a small bothy (1hr 40mins).

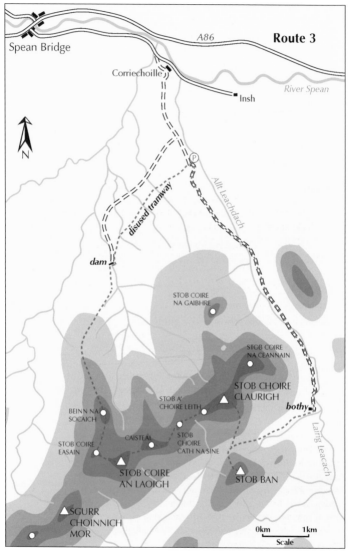

The surface rock of the Grey Corries is mainly a shattered grey-white quartzite, which gives the covering of scree from which the hills get their collective name. From a distance they seem to be shrouded in a pale grey cloth or a capping of snow. The extensive screes on these hills have been formed since the last Ice Age by the repeated action of water freezing and thawing; the water expands like a wedge in tiny crevices in the rock, shattering it into ever-smaller pieces. The whole area has also been subjected to extensive geological folding.

There is no doubt that the best way to experience the excellent ridge walking of the Grey Corries is to climb them in a single expedition, starting at Corriechoille and finishing at Glen Nevis (23km, 8hrs 15mins). This provides a superb day's walking, covering the whole length of the ridge, with no technical difficulties on the way and fairly easy route-finding as most of the ridge is well defined. There are some fine situations and good views throughout, weather permitting. However this does require the use of a vehicle at either end of the walk, or perhaps the help of an accommodating driver, and for this reason I have split the ridge into two walks here. True, it would be possible to tackle the ridge in one outing from Corriechoille, going as far as Sgurr Choinnich Mor, then returning back along the ridge to the starting point, but this would make for a very long and arduous day, with the need to regain a lot of height over Stob Coire Easain late in the day. If you cannot arrange for transport in Glen Nevis, it would be better to tackle Sgurr Choinnich Mor separately from Glen Nevis on another day, giving two good outings instead of one.

One route from here crosses the Allt a' Chuil Choirean then climbs the northeast spur of Stob Ban. However, when the river is full it is much easier to follow its heathery north bank and head in a west-southwesterly direction straight up to the col between Stob Ban and Stob Coire Claurigh. The final slopes are grassy and quite steep, and lead to a small lochan. This lochan, marked on the map at 26519 72851, is obvious when you have found it; however after heavy rainfall there are one or two small pools just before you reach it, which may lead to confusion. From the lochan head south-southwest over an undulating ridge until the path steepens over scree and blocks to reach **Stob Ban** summit at 26652 72402 (3hrs).

The Grey Corries, with Stob Coire Easain on right

Retrace your steps to the lochan then head north up a broad ridge, veering off to the northwest at about 26466 73683 where grey quartzite blocks begin to litter the hillside. The cairned summit of **Stob Choire Claurigh** is at 26209 73862 (4hrs).

The ridge leads off to the southwest from here and is well-defined throughout most of its length, as is the undulating pinky-grey path along its crest. It may not be easy in poor weather, however, to identify exactly where you are on the ridge. The path crosses a couple of minor tops and passes a cairned top at 25238 73038 before reaching another cairn on a rocky top known as Caisteal ('the castle') at 24670 72929 (this is Point 1104 on the OS map). The ridge narrows here, then passes another small cairn before reaching the summit of **Stob Coire an Laoigh** at 23994 72513, where there is a small enclosure of stones. Continue west-northwest to the summit of Stob Coire Easain at 23480 72728 (5hrs 20mins).

If you are continuing on the ridge and descending into Glen Nevis, head southwest from here over Sgurr Choinnich Mor and Sgurr Choinnich Beag, reversing Route 4. If you are returning to the day's starting point, turn north along the broad north ridge of Stob Coire Easain. Pass over Beinn na Socaich and continue descending to the north to about Point 23298 74692 before veering north-northeast. Veering off too soon will lead you onto crags on the east side of the ridge. The Allt Choimhlidh river must next be crossed. Descend a very steep grass slope close to the edge of the forest where there is a dam across the river. Unfortunately it is not possible to cross via the dam itself, but the river can most easily be crossed a few metres in front of the dam. There is a stile at the far side of the dam which leads via a walkway to a forest track. This emerges some way below the tramway and takes you back to the main track between Corriechoille and your starting point. A more direct way back is to climb the embankment on the other side of the river and descend through a clearing in the trees to reach the rather muddy line of the old tramway, which can be followed directly back to the car parking area. The rails of the tramway have been long-since removed and only a few sleepers and the broken remains of one or two bridges now remain.

ROUTE 4

Sgurr Choinnich Mor (1094m)

Pronunciation: Skoor Chorneech More
Translation: Big Peak of the Moss

Distance:	16km
Ascent:	1020m
Time:	6hrs
Maps:	OS sheet 41; Explorer map 392; Harvey's Superwalker map Ben Nevis; Area Map 1; see Route 2 for sketch map
Parking:	car park at the end of Glen Nevis
Start:	from the east end of car park follow footpath through Nevis gorge
Hostel:	YHA Glen Nevis; Independent Glen Nevis
B&B/hotel:	Glen Nevis, Fort William
Camping:	Glen Nevis campsite
Access:	Bidwells, tel: 01397 702433

This pleasant walk starts along the Water of Nevis and takes you up to the most westerly peaks of the Grey Corries.

The approach to Sgurr Choinnich Mor from Glen Nevis is a sheer delight, following the spectacular path along the water of Nevis past the picturesque waterfall at Steall. Continue over a wooden bridge and past the ruins for a further 2km to a point where the path becomes vague at 20457 68876 (1hr 15mins).

From here, strike up the rough grassy hillside in a northeasterly direction, picking out the easiest line. There are traces of a path for a while but this quickly peters out. A small waterfall about halfway up the slope can be passed on either side. You should emerge eventually just below the steeper slopes of Sgurr Choinnich Beag at 21662 70686. Climb quite steeply northeast up a narrowing ridge to the summit at 22014 71014 (3hrs 20mins).

The Grey Corries from col between Aonach Mor and Aonach Beag

Aonach Beag from Sgur Choinnich Beag

Descend to a col to the east of Sgurr Choinnich Beag and continue up to the summit of its slightly higher neighbour, **Sgurr Choinnich Mor**. The summit cairn is at 22771 71408, and from here, weather permitting, you'll get wonderful views of the rocky bastions of the Aonachs to the west and the shapely peaks of the Mamores to the south (3hrs 50mins).

Return by the same route.

THE MAMORES

ROUTE 5
Mullach nan Coirean (939m), Stob Ban (999m), Sgurr a' Mhaim (1099m)

Pronunciation: *Mooluch nuh Yerrigen; Stob Ban; Skoor uh Vime*
Translation: *Summit of the Corries; White Peak; Peak of the Round Hill*

Distance:	15km
Ascent:	1470m
Time:	7hrs
Difficulty:	exposed section on the Devil's Ridge – may become dangerous in high wind
Maps:	OS sheet 41; Explorer map 392; Harvey's Superwalker map Ben Nevis; Area Map 1
Parking:	car park by the bridge at Polldubh
Start:	footpath from road opposite the buildings at Polldubh
Camping:	Glen Nevis campsite
Hostel:	YHA Glen Nevis; Independent Glen Nevis
B&B/hotel:	Glen Nevis, Fort William
Access:	hillphone: 01855 831511

This classic walk crosses three Munros and incorporates a wonderful variety of scenery and some excellent ridge walking, including the deliciously exposed Devil's Ridge.

Rubbing shoulders with the great mountain mass of Ben Nevis to the north and the grandeur of the Aonach Eagach and the Glencoe hills to the south, the Mamores promise much. They don't disappoint. The 10 Munros and seven tops of this range can be tackled equally well from the Glen Nevis side or from Kinlochleven, and can be grouped together in many different ways to provide excellent ridge walking on red granite and interfolded white quartzite and schists. Deep corries fall away from the ridges at every turn. Fell runners will do all the peaks in a single day. Mere mortals will be happy to take longer. The range is split here into three superb outings, one from the Glen Nevis side and the other two from Kinlochleven, allowing the entire ridge to be covered in three days without undue strain.

Opposite the buildings at Polldubh a gated forestry track winds gently up the hillside. Starting to the left of the track, at 14238 68360, a footpath takes a more direct

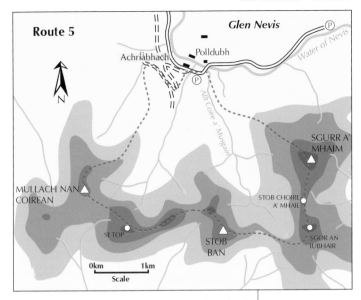

Route 5

Glen Nevis

Achríabhach

Polldubh

Water of Nevis

Allt Coire a' Mhusgain

SGURR A' MHAIM

MULLACH NAN COIREAN

STOB CHOIRE A' MHAIL

SE TOP

STOB BAN

SGOR AN IUBHAIR

0km   1km
Scale

line, rejoining the track just before its second sharp bend. Go around this bend and stay on the track through the forest, passing the next junction, until the track is barred by a stream. A footpath winds pleasantly up to the left of the stream and this is followed to a fence. Follow the line of the fence, crossing it at a stile, onto open rising ground. By the time the fence turns abruptly east at 13143 67128, the northeast ridge of Mullach is clearly defined and the path is followed on its crest, past a cairned top at 12325 66513, to **Mullach nan Coirean**'s main summit at 12238 66218 (2hrs).

Head southeast from the summit cairn until the round granite dome of Mullach narrows to a ridge once again. The ridge then rises over the South Top (13115 65470), followed by the white quartzite of another minor top (13911 65792) before veering south to the summit of **Stob Ban**, which is capped by Binnean quartzite (14778 65437) (3hrs 30mins).

From the summit of Stob Ban head south for 50m to pick up the path on the east ridge. The start (cairned) drops down quite abruptly. This path is followed right down the ridge until it crosses a stalker's path coming up from the Old Military Road. Taking the north fork of this crossing will take you directly back to Polldubh. Instead, cross over this path to reach a little lochan which feeds the Allt Coire a' Mhusgain. Here the ways diverge: one path passing to the north of the lochan rises directly to Stob Choire a' Mhail; the other, passing to its south, leads to Sgor an Iubhair, which until 1997 was accorded the status of a Munro in its own right. It is worth taking in this extra top; to do so take the path to the southeast. After a short distance this path splits at 15969 65273. Take the left branch and work your way up the block-strewn landscape to the summit at 16526 65506 (4hrs 40mins).

Leaving the summit to the northwest, the ridge soon narrows to a knife-edged arête – this is the Devil's Ridge. There are no particularly difficult moves on this section unless the path is banked with snow, but it provides a wonderful airy walk with exposure on both sides. Route-finding here is not a problem. If you think you've lost the path, check your altitude: you may just

Sgurr a' Mhaim (Mamores) from Glen Nevis

have fallen a few hundred metres. The path rises over a minor top, Stob Choire a' Mhail, before eventually reaching the broad quartzite flanks of **Sgurr a' Mhaim** (16466 66724) (5hrs 10mins).

The whole of Sgurr a' Mhaim, which sits on a bed of schist, has been affected by a massive landslip in what are, geologically speaking, quite recent times. Making sure you avoid any slips of your own, descend to the northwest on white quartzite scree and chippings. These soon peter out and from this point on the path descends gently at first, then much more steeply back to Polldubh. Those with weak knees might prefer to do this circuit in the opposite direction as the descent from Sgurr a' Mhaim is a bone-jarring exercise at the end of a long day. On the other hand many might feel that ascending such a path first thing in the morning is an unsavoury way to start the day.

ROUTE 6

*Na Gruagaichean (1055m),
An Gearanach (982m), Stob Coire
a' Chairn (981m), Am Bodach (1032m)*

*Pronunciation: Na Grooageechan;
Un Gearahnoch; Stob Korrer a Charn; Am Bottoch*
*Translation: The Maidens; the Complainer;
Peak of the Corrie of the Cairn; the Old Man*

An excellent walk, albeit a fairly tough one, crossing four Munros. The ridge to An Gearanach involves some pleasant, easy scrambling and is quite exposed in places.

From Mamore Lodge take the Landrover track which contours the valley of the Allt Coire na Bà. Just where it swings round to the south, a footpath leads onto the open

Distance:	15km
Ascent:	1400m
Time:	8hrs
Difficulty:	some exposure on section between An Garbanach and An Gearanach, which also involves some easy scrambling (grade 1) – could become dangerous in high wind
Maps:	OS sheet 41; Explorer map 392; Harvey's Superwalker map Ben Nevis; Area Map 1
Parking:	lay-by near start of estate road by Lochleven (free). Car park (small charge) at Mamore Lodge. Cars should not be driven onto estate roads beyond the lodge.
Start:	along private track from Mamore Lodge
Camping:	Kinlochleven
Hostel:	YHA Glencoe; Independent bunkhouse at Kinlochleven campsite
B&B/hotel:	Kinlochleven
Access:	hillphone: 01855 831511

hill. Follow the path along the burn as it climbs gently into the upper reaches of the corrie. When it reaches steeper ground the path swings round to the east and then heads almost south beneath the summit of Na Gruagaichean. Eventually it doubles back at 19691 64958 towards Stob Coire a' Chairn. At this point you leave it and strike out due east straight up the hill, to the right of a small depression, climbing over quartzite blocks to arrive just south of the main top of **Na Gruagaichean**. Continue up to the summit cairn (2hrs 30mins).

A gentle ridge curves round to Binnein Mor to the northeast from here; however, your route heads northwest, dropping steeply from the summit to arrive at a beallach. This grassy ridge leads eventually on to the stony summit of Stob Coire a' Chairn. Follow it for a while, but as you will return over this peak later in the day, it is pointless to go all the way now. Instead take a little path that leads off the ridge to the right at 19162 65801 and contour around the northeastern slopes of

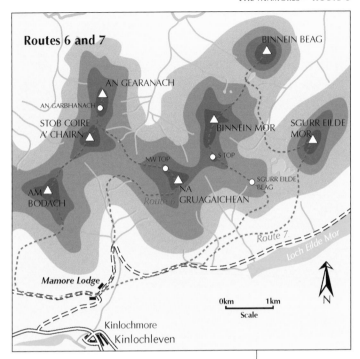

Stob Coire a' Chairn, crossing a small burn to arrive on the ridge between Stob Coire a' Chairn and An Garbhanach. (Neither of these peaks is named on the older 1:50,000 OS maps.) From here climb the rocky slopes of An Garbanach (18830 66532), then cross a fairly exposed and rocky section of the ridge, which involves some easy scrambling, to reach the summit cairn of **An Gearanach** at 18776 66978 (4hrs 15mins).

From An Gearanach a tortuous path leads north and drops steeply down to Steall Bridge in Glen Nevis. However you have two more summits awaiting, so retrace your steps back over An Garbanach (it's a pleasure to do this little section again in the opposite direction) and continue along the ridge to reach the

An Gearanach and the Mamores from Sgurr Choinnich Mor

quartzite summit of **Stob Coire a' Chairn** at 18587 66124 (5hrs 10mins).

From the summit cairn head west, then southwest to reach the steep loose path (awkward in descent) that climbs the northeast buttress of **Am Bodach**, your final Munro of the day, at 17639 65084 (5hrs 55mins).

From the main top, go southeast for about 100m to a subsidiary cairn and then continue along the ridge towards Sgorr an Fhuarain. The southern slopes of Sgorr an Fhuarain are steep and craggy, but the western flanks of the ridge are heathery and much more gentle. Before reaching Sgorr an Fhuarain, at about 17945 64534, start the descent, heading for a stalker's path at 17246 64397, where it crosses the burn. Follow this path easily back to the Landrover track and so to Mamore Lodge.

ROUTE 7

Sgurr Eilde Mor (1010m),

Binnein Beag (943m),

Binnein Mor (1130m)

Pronunciation: Skoor
Edge-yer More; Beenyan Bake; Beenyan More
Translation: Small Peak; Big Peak; Big Peak of the Hind

Distance:	18km
Ascent:	1620m
Time:	9hrs
Difficulty:	short section of easy scrambling (up to grade 1) on the northeast ridge of Binnein Mor
Maps:	OS sheet 41; Explorer map 392; Harvey's Superwalker map Ben Nevis; Area Map 1; see Route 6 for sketch map
Parking:	lay-by near start of estate road by Lochleven (free); car park (small charge) Mamore Lodge
Start:	along private track from Mamore Lodge
Camping:	Kinlochleven
Hostel:	YHA Glencoe; Independent Kinlochleven campsite.
B&B/hotel:	Kinlochleven
Access:	hillphone: 01855 831511

This is a long route into the remote mountain landscape at the eastern end of the Mamores. Access is aided by an estate track for part of the way, but some of the route – particularly over Sgurr Eilde Mor – is over very rough terrain. Some easy scrambling is involved on the northeast ridge of Binnein Mor.

Starting from Mamore Lodge take the Landrover track to Loch Eilde Mor. A footpath offers a shortcut across the big loop in the track around the Allt Coire na Bà. After 3½km

59

at 22220 63786 a path leads onto the hill and this is followed all the way to the Coire an Lochain. From the lochan climb up the south-southwest spur of **Sgurr Eilde Mor** over a jumble of blocks to the summit at 23051 65772 (3hrs).

A ridge leads off from the top to the west and this is followed, bearing right after 200m. Drop down on the shattered quartz until the path winds past Coire an Lochain and crosses the infant burn, the Allt Coire a' Bhinnein. Then follow the contours of Binnein Mor as the path winds its way to the lochan between Binnein Mor and Binnein Beag at 21889 67120. It is a straightforward climb from this lochan up the little **Binnein Beag** to its remote summit at 22178 67706 (5hrs).

To descend, retrace your steps to the lochan. Do not be tempted to take the well-used scree slope that drops steeply and unpleasantly to the west of the path. From the lochan begin the long climb of **Binnein Mor**, the highest peak in the Mamore chain. Head directly up the steep northeast ridge over grass, then schistose blocks until you come to a break in the ridge. The curved rocks of the

The Mamores from Sgurr Choinnich Mor (Sgurr Eilde Mor on left)

The eastern Mamores from Coire na Tulaich

summit ridge have a forbidding look from afar, but as you approach them their angle recedes. Tackle the rocks straight up the middle. There are good big holds all the way up and the rock is sound. You emerge on the sharp summit crest at 21219 66344 (6hrs 30mins)

Traverse along the main ridge to a minor top at 21109 65686, then descend the southeast spur to Sgor Eilde Beag. The way off finds a line down the very steep nose of this spur, and it is important here to locate the path. There is a cairn marking its start at 22044 65018. This clear path goes across the moor and rejoins the Landrover track beneath Na Gruagaichean and from here it is an easy trek back to Mamore Lodge.

LOCH TREIG

ROUTE 8

Stob a Choire Mheadoin (1105m),
Stob Coire Easain (1115m)

Pronunciation: *Stob a Horrer Veeyann; Stob Korrer Essin*
Translation: *Peak of the Middle Corrie;*
Peak of the Corrie of the Little Waterfall

Distance:	15km
Ascent:	1020m
Time:	5hrs 30mins (a little longer if returning by the north ridge of Stob Coire Easain to the old tramway)
Maps:	OS sheet 41; Explorer maps 392 and 393; Harvey's Superwalker map Ben Nevis; Area Map 1
Parking:	parking area just to the west of Fersit at 34997 78158
Start:	south along private works track from the car park
Hostel:	Independent Hostels at Inverroy and Tulloch station; YHA Glen Nevis and Loch Lochy
B&B/hotel:	Roy Bridge
Camping:	Inverroy
Access:	Bidwells, tel: 01397 702433

The ridge to the west of Loch Treig offers this fairly straightforward walk taking in two Munros and giving good views of the Grey Corries and surrounding hills.

There are several ways of getting onto the main ridge. One rather boggy path leads directly onto the slopes of Creag Fhiaclach from the car park, emerging on the crest of the ridge further south, but the best route (that is the

These two summits are the highest points of the long ridge that stretches along the west side of Loch Treig. Good views of the ridge can be had from the train on the other side of the loch when travelling between Tulloch and Corrour. The ridge forms part of the Loch Treig schist and quartzite formation, and the predominant rock is a white micaceous quartzite, covered on the lower slopes by thick peat. About 7km east of Roy Bridge a minor road leaves the A86 and winds its way to Fersit, crossing en route an alarmingly labelled 'weak bridge' and an even weaker-looking wooden bridge. Cars may be left in the opening at 34997 78158 just before the houses are reached.

easiest and least boggy) is to take the old works track to the dam at the outflow of Loch Treig. Where the track branches just above the dam take the right fork. Continue on the track until a path leads off to the right (west) at 34483 76936. This path heads west, then southwest across a grassy slope and leads up to a prominent concrete pillar on the skyline. (The direct path from the car park rejoins it at this point.) Once on the broad ridge, head straight for the steep nose of Meall Cian Dearg. A path zigzags straight up the nose, tending slightly to the

Stob Coire Easain and Stob á Choire Mheadhoin from Coire na Tulaich

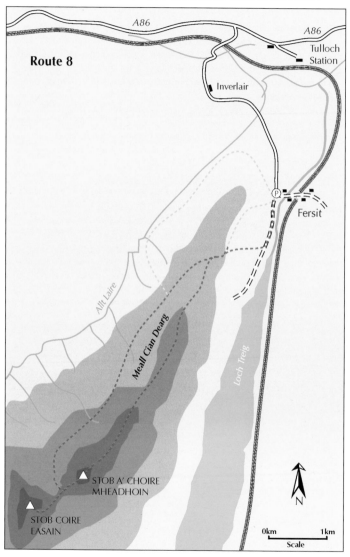

west, to emerge on a flattish plateau at 33140 75792 (1hr 40mins).

Continue south-southwest, then southwest along the broad ridge which rises onto a second undulating plateau, past a small cairn of no significance, until a final stony climb takes you to the conical top of **Stob a' Choire Mheadhoin** at 31657 73633 (2hrs 50mins).

From the summit cairn there are fine views across to Stob Ban and the Grey Corries. Continue to the south-west, dropping to a col between Stob a' Choire Mheadhoin and Stob Coire Easain, then climb the steep little ridge that leads to the top of **Stob Coire Easain** at 30807 73065 (3hrs 20mins).

There are various possibilities for the return journey. Some parties simply retrace their steps back over Stob a' Choire Mheadhoin and Meall Cian Dearg. It is also possible to descend the north ridge of Stob Coire Easain to Coire Laire (steep in places) then walk back along the river. If descending this way it is necessary to make sure you have cleared all the cliffs on the east side of this ridge before veering round to the northeast. Perhaps a more popular way back is to return to the col between Stob Coire Easain and Stob a' Choire Mheadhoin and at 31278 73215 descend steeply to the northwest. There is a path at first, which then disappears briefly over rocks to reappear again lower down. It is worth finding the path again if you have lost it, for it hugs the slopes of Stob a' Choire Mheadhoin staying quite high on the hill, well away from the river and the wet ground below. Eventually the path splits. One branch goes down to join a track by the Allt Laire just before it goes into woodland, then links up with the line of the old tramway around the nose of Creag Ghiaclach to find its way back to the car park. The other branch goes northeast under the nose of Meall Cian Dearg to rejoin the outward route just before the concrete pillar.

ROUTE 9

Stob Coire Sgriodain (979m),

Chno Dearg (1046m)

Pronunciation: *Stob Korrer Skreethane; Knorr Jerrack*
Translation: *Peak of the Corrie of the Scree; Red Hill*

Distance:	13km
Ascent:	940m
Time:	5hrs
Maps:	OS sheet 41; Explorer map 393; Area Map 1
Parking:	parking area just west of Fersit
Start:	east along public road through Fersit
Hostel:	Independent Hostels at Roy Bridge and Tulloch Station; YHA Glen Nevis and Loch Lochy
B&B/hotel:	Roy Bridge and Spean Bridge
Camping:	Roy Bridge
Access:	Forest Enterprise, tel: 01397 702185 or hillphone: 01397 732200

These two Munros give a fairly short and straightforward walk without any great difficulty.

Start from the car parking area at 34997 78158, just before the houses are reached, as for the previous route. Beyond this point the road is private. Continue on foot through Fersit, crossing the bridge and passing the small settlement until the road turns into a track which is gated. Pass through the gate and take the track marked 'to Corrour Station'. Turn off this track after a short distance at 36065 77845 onto a farm trail which makes for easy progress through some wet and boggy land. This trail continues high up into a corrie beneath Stob Coire Sgriodain, but there is no access to the peak from here,

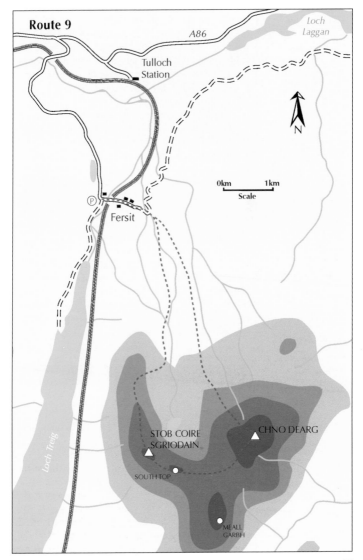

Route 9

A86

Loch Laggan

Tulloch Station

N

0km   1km
Scale

P
Fersit

Loch Treig

STOB COIRE SGRIODAIN

CHNO DEARG

SOUTH TOP

MEALL GARBH

so the trail has to be left after 1½km. Head for an obvious grassy ramp at 35843 75869 that climbs the nose of Sron na Garbh-bheinne. Climb the ramp, tending left, to gain the ridge proper and the minor top. From here the ridge rises to the south until the cairned summit of **Stob Coire Sgriodain** is reached at 35675 74397 (2hrs 15mins).

Continue south for a few hundred metres, dropping to a col. The next section rises and falls over a number of small undulations. Continue south for another couple of hundred metres before changing direction to the south-east. Changing too soon will lead to steeper terrain and the need to regain lost height unnecessarily. A subsidiary top is crossed at 35940 73875 (Point 958) and from here a southeasterly course will bring you to a second minor top at 36406 73641 (Point 924). A detour can be made after this to Meall Garbh for those wishing to take in an extra top. Alternatively, follow an easterly course to reach the rounded slopes of **Chno Dearg** 37166 73669 and then veer northeast to reach its flat, boulder-strewn summit at 37742 74106 (3hrs 30mins).

The descent is simple, heading north-northwest down a slope that is bouldery, then grassy, then wet, until the farm trail is picked up back to Fersit.

ARDVERIKIE

ROUTE 10
*Beinn a' Chlachair (1087m), Geal Charn
(1049m), Creag Pitridh (924m)*

Pronunciation: *Bine uh Chlachear;
Geeya Charn; Krayk Peetree*
Translation: *Stonemason's Hill; Pale Hill; Petrie's Crag*

From the lay-by midway between Moy and Moy Lodge, cross the River Spean on the private road, bearing left

Distance:	26km
Ascent:	1310m
Time:	8hrs 30mins (1hr can be saved if using a bike on the estate roads)
Maps:	OS sheet 42; Explorer map 393; Area Map 1
Parking:	lay-by on A86 at 43310 83019
Start:	head south along a private track leading off A86 – this starts just west of lay-by
Hostel:	Independent Hostels at Tulloch and Roy Bridge; YHA Glen Nevis and Loch Lochy
B&B/hotel:	Inverroy; Roy Bridge
Camping:	Inverroy; Roy Bridge
Access:	Ardverikie Estate, tel: 01528 544300

Sitting some way back from the A86, these three Munros make for a long and fairly tough day's walking. This is partly on account of the long approach along the estate track and partly on account of the liberal covering of blocks and stones on most of the high ground, which makes for slow and sometimes tedious progress. Fortunately this is more than made up for by the views.

after 300m, and follow the track to a T-junction. Take the right turn here and skirt around the southwestern end of Binnean Shuas (the left turn goes through woods to the southern shores of Loch Laggan). The track forks again after another 1½km. This time the right fork leads up to the Allt Cam and from here it is possible to make an ascent of Beinn a' Chlachair's west ridge. This makes a natural circuit around the three hills, though it is a somewhat longer route than the more usual approach, which is from the Allt Coire Pitridh. For the more direct approach take the left fork at the junction, which leads past one small lochan to a larger one – the Lochan na h-Earba – and eventually takes you onto the northern flanks of Beinn a' Chlachair. Pass the golden sandy beaches at the southwestern end of Lochan na h-Earba and take to

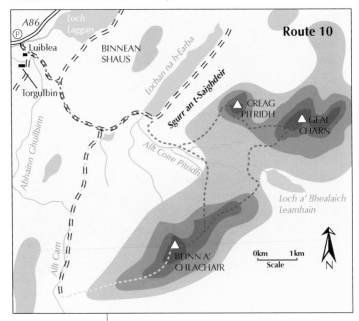

the stalker's path that leads from here alongside the Allt Coire Pitridh. After 1½–2km leave this path and head south to the grassy banks of Beinn a' Chlachair (2hrs 25mins).

The exact point of ascent does not matter too much, as long as the big corrie, Coire Mor Chlachair, is avoided. Once on the main ridge head southwest, passing around the rim of the Coire Mor Chlachair to reach the **Beinn a' Chlachair** summit cairn at 47128 78143 (3hrs 45mins).

To reach **Geal Charn** head back along the block-strewn ridge for nearly 3km to reach its northeastern end and descend over rocks, staying to the left of any real difficulties. This brings you back to the stalker's path which is followed downhill for a couple of hundred metres to a fork. Take the right fork and head north for ½km before striking uphill to the northeast. This broad ridge is also covered in blocks of stone, and the summit

can seem a long time coming. The cairn is reached at 50431 81183, after a couple of undulations in the summit dome have been crossed. It is not the easiest of targets in very thick weather (5hrs 45mins).

Beinn a' Chlachair from the north

Retrace your steps to reach the path that crosses the col between Geal Charn and Creag Pitridh. It is important to pass to the south of an area of steep rocks on the western side of Geal Charn, so in poor visibility give these a wide berth and go to 49253 80872 before turning northwest to reach the path at 49132 80990. From here cross the col and follow the path up the southwestern side of **Creag Pitridh**, before veering back to its summit at 48745 81453 (6hrs 35mins).

From the summit cairn head west, then southwest, picking up a path that leads down grassy slopes to the Allt Coire Pitridh. The path peters out after a while but the gentle slopes to the south and east of Sgurr an t-Saighdeir lead easily down to the stalker's path along the Allt Coire Pitridh. From the Lochan na h-Earba the estate road takes you back to the start.

LOCH OSSIAN

ROUTE 11
Beinn Eibhinn (1102m),
Aonach Beag (1116m)

Pronunciation: Bine Eh-veen; Ernoch Bake
Translation: Delightful Mountain; Wee Ridged Peak

Distance:	29km (of which 14km is on estate roads)
Ascent:	1140m
Time:	8hrs 30mins (2hrs less if a bike is used on the estate tracks)
Maps:	OS sheets 41 and 42; Explorer maps 393 and 385; Area Map 1
Parking:	cars may be left at Rannoch or Tulloch stations. There is no vehicular access for the general public to the Loch Ossian area.
Start:	track leads east from Corrour station
Hostel:	YHA Loch Ossian; Independent bunkhouse at Corrour station has now reopened
B&B/hotel:	Roy Bridge
Camping:	no campsites in immediate area; camping at Roy Bridge
Access:	Forest Enterprise, tel: 01397 702185. Hillphone, tel: 01397 732200. Ben Alder Estate (if approached from the east), tel: 01528 522224

From the station follow the track along the south side of Loch Ossian. At the east end of the loch the track turns north, crossing a bridge at the outflow of the loch at 41261 69652 (1hr 20mins walking).

On the far side of this bridge a path leads off to the right. Follow this to the footbridge over the Uisge Labhair. The path continues on the north side of the Uisge Labhair, crossing a tributary burn, the Allt Feith a' Mheallein. Continue on for another ½km to Point 43187 70361 before heading north up the slopes of Meall Glas Choire. Turning off the path too soon lands you in wet

These two remote hills, shouldered between the Ardverikie Munros and the mighty Ben Alder, lie in the middle of a wild and beautiful mountain part of the central Highlands that few visitors ever get to see. The walk divides into two contrasting parts: a long, level approach on the estate track alongside Loch Ossian and a climb from the outflow of the loch to reach the two summits.

These hills could perhaps be approached from Loch Laggan in the north with a long walk-in along the Allt Cam, but they are usually tackled either from the east via Culra Bothy, by extending the route over Geal Charn and Carn Dearg, or from the west, starting from Corrour as described here. All of these approaches require a long walk-in, and whichever starting-point is chosen for the ascent, a mountain bike will eat up the long kilometres of the estate roads in a most welcome manner.

Those who can't do without their creature comforts will find there is enough time between the first and last trains from Corrour station to complete Beinn Eibhinn and Aonach Beag and return to the fleshpots of Fort William the same day. Strong parties might even include Beinn na Lap in time for the return train in the evening. If you stay at Loch Ossian hostel, or if you use a bike for the estate roads, then Beinn na Lap can easily be included in the day's outing.

terrain, which is cut up by a fan of small streams feeding the Uisge Labhair. Climb the slopes over a small top, Creagan na Craoibhe, to the larger top, Meall Glas Choire, at 43647 72776 (3hrs 25mins).

Descend briefly to the north to a small col, then climb the grassy slopes of Beinn Eibhinn's western top. It isn't necessary to go quite to the top, but it doesn't matter if you do. At 43940 73431 turn east, passing two small lochans, and follow the rising ridge which veers round to the southeast until the summit of **Beinn Eibhinn** is reached at 44824 73375 (4hrs 5mins).

Continue past a secondary cairn until the curving ridge narrows and falls to a col, then rises again to the summit of **Aonach Beag** at 45790 74178 (4hrs 35mins).

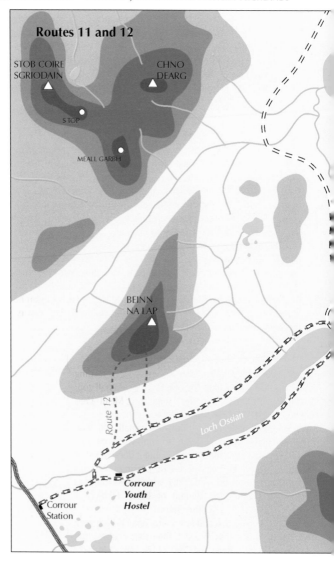

Routes 11 and 12

STOB COIRE
SGRIODAIN
△

CHNO
DEARG
△

S TOP ○

MEALL GARBH ○

BEINN
NA LAP
△

Route 12

Loch Ossian

Corrour
Youth
Hostel

Corrour
Station

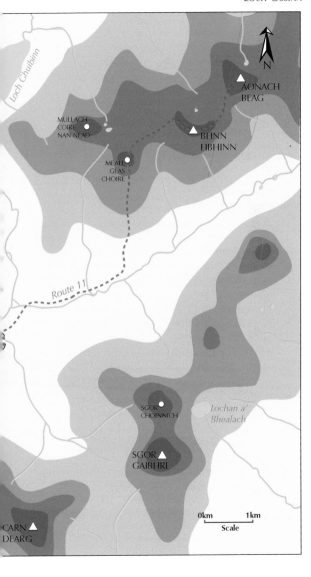

75

It is necessary to recross Beinn Eibhinn on the return, as there are no safe shortcuts. Return by the same route.

ROUTE 12

Beinn na Lap (935m)

Pronunciation: *Bine na Lap*
Translation: *Dappled Hill*

Distance:	9km (33km if done in conjunction with Beinn Eibhinn and Aonach Beag)
Ascent:	570m
Time:	3hrs 15mins from Corrour station (10hrs 45mins if combined with above route, though 2hrs can be saved if a bike is used to cover the estate tracks)
Maps:	OS sheet 41; Explorer map 385; Area Map 1; see Route 11 for sketch map
Parking:	cars may be left at Tulloch or Rannoch stations; there is no vehicular access to the Loch Ossian area
Start:	track leads east from Corrour station (or the route can be combined with Route 11)
Hostel:	YHA Loch Ossian; Independent bunkhouse at Corrour station
B&B/hotel:	this excursion can be made from any of the stops between Fort William and Glasgow
Camping:	none in the immediate area; camping at Roy Bridge
Access:	Forest Enterprise, tel: 01397 702185. Hillphone: 01397 732200

Beinn na Lap is one of the easiest Munros to climb, despite the fact that it is quite a long way from the nearest road.

On its own this hill is an easy morning's walk from Corrour Station. From the station take the Loch Ossian track, turning left after 1200m to skirt the northern shores of the loch. Continue on the track for 1km before heading uphill over rough grassland. **Beinn na Lap** can also be combined with the route above by returning from Beinn Eibhinn along the north side of Loch Ossian. From this direction stay on the track for ½km after the track leaves the trees, then head uphill to reach a stile. A high deer fence follows the 450m contour around this part of the hill, and from either direction it is necessary to cross this at one of the specially constructed stiles. Aim for the stile at 37278 68012, then head north straight up the rough slope, veering northeast towards the top. There is a well-built stone enclosure on the first top reached, but the highest point is a little further on, past a small lochan, at 37620 69573 (2hrs from Corrour).

Return by the same route to the stile, then continue on the estate road, turning right at the junction to reach Corrour station, or left to arrive at the atmospheric little youth hostel beside Loch Ossian.

ROUTE 13

Carn Dearg (941m), Sgor Gaibhre (955m)

Pronunciation: *Karn Jerrack; Skor Gay-yerrer*
Translation: *Red Hill; Peak of the Goats*

To the south of Loch Ossian lie these two fairly straightforward Munros. It should be possible to climb them from Corrour station between the morning train from Fort William and the return train in the afternoon. Alternatively, Loch Ossian's prize-winning 'green' hostel makes an excellent base for the area.

Follow the track from the station to Loch Ossian, taking the right fork where the path divides. If you are cycling, continue to GR 39603 67779, about 1½km beyond the start of a plantation. Leave bikes here and cut uphill through scattered trees to find a path that skirts around

Distance:	22km
Ascent:	790m
Time:	5hrs 55mins (1hr less if a bike is used on the estate track)
Maps:	OS sheets 41 and 42; Explorer map 385; Area Map 1
Parking:	no vehicular access to this area; arrive at Corrour station by train
Start:	estate track from Corrour station along south side of Loch Ossian
Hostel:	YHA Corrour; Independent station bunkhouse
B&B/hotel:	none in the immediate area, but this excursion can be done from any of the stops on the line between Glasgow and Fort William
Camping:	no sites in the immediate area; camping at Roy Bridge
Access:	Forest Enterprise, tel: 01397 702185. Hillphone: 01397 732200

the upper edge of the plantation. Pass Peter's Rock then branch uphill to the left over heathery moorland. If you set out from the station on foot, leave the track just south of the youth hostel on a path that leads to the same point. Continue uphill to a broad col. There is a faint path on

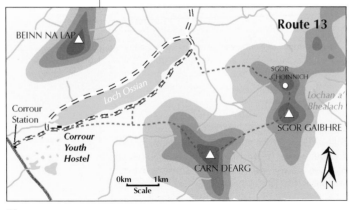

the north side of a small burn – the infant Allt a' Choire Odhair Bhig – but finding it is not really necessary. Aim for the centre of the col, and once this is gained turn right (south) along the ridge, rising easily to the stony summit of **Carn Dearg** with its prominent cairn at 41777 66136 (2hrs 20mins).

Head down a rather broken ridge to the wide col between Carn Dearg and Sgor Gaibhre then climb easily up to **Sgor Gaibhre** summit at 44473 67431 (3hrs 20mins). There are excellent views across Rannoch Moor to Schiehallion from this vantage point.

To descend, drop down quite steeply but easily to another col to the north, then either climb the minor top of Sgor Choinnich or skirt around its left (west) flank and follow its northwest ridge gently down to its end at a small cairn on Meall Nathrach Mor, then after quite a steep drop initially, go down grass and heather slopes to the west to reach a small dam on the Allt a' Choire Chreagaich. Cross the burn here to join a track that goes through the trees and back to Loch Ossian past the estate buildings. When it is in spate it may not be possible to cross at the dam, in which case return to the loch along the east side of the burn. Return to the starting point along the track that skirts the southern shores of the loch.

BEN ALDER

ROUTE 14
Ben Alder (1148m), Beinn Bheoil (1019m)

Pronunciation: Ben Alder; Bine Vee-awl
Translation: (possibly) Mountain of the
Water of the Steep Slope; Mountain of the Mouth

It is possible to cycle in to Culra Bothy, do this route, and then cycle out in a single day. Many people, however, will prefer to use the bothy as a base and stay to do other hills in the area. Walkers should satisfy themselves that

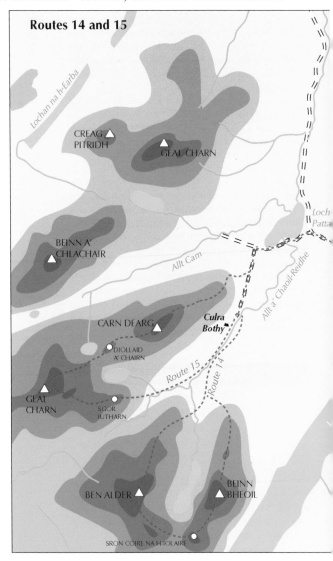

Routes 14 and 15

Lochan na h-Earba

CREAG PITRIDH

GEAL CHARN

Loch Patta

BEINN A' CHLACHAIR

Allt Cam

Allt a' Chaoil-Reidhe

CARN DEARG

Culra Bothy

DIOLLAID A' CHAIRN

Route 15

Route 14

GEAL CHARN

SGOR IUTHARN

BEN ALDER

BEINN BHEOIL

SRON COIRE NA H-IOLAIRE

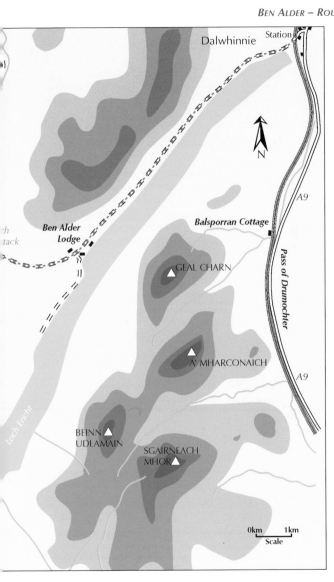

In fine weather this is one of Scotland's classic walks, involving a long excursion in the remote heart of the Highlands, far from any road, with glorious mountain scenery all around and continual interest throughout the walk. Bonnie Prince Charlie spent time in these hills, hiding in a remote bothy to the south of Ben Alder. It is little wonder he spent his later years in exile dreaming and reminiscing about the heather-clad hills of Scotland.

they have the necessary permission from Network Rail to use the railway crossing at Dalwhinnie. (Failing this there is a bridge under the line about ½km south – turn off the A889 by a garage.) An alternative approach, which is roughly the same distance, starts from the A86 just east of Loch Laggan. An estate track can be followed from here to Loch Pattack.

Distance:	48km from Dalwhinnie (of which 32km can be cycled); 16km if starting and finishing at Culra
Ascent:	970m
Time:	13hrs 30mins walking from Dalwhinnie (5hrs less if a bike is used on estate tracks). 5hrs 30mins if starting and finishing at Culra
Difficulty:	some simple scrambling (grade 0.5)
Maps:	OS sheet 42; Explorer map 393; Area Map 1
Parking:	south of Dalwhinnie railway station at railway crossing – marked 'parking area'
Start:	cross the railway line (see 'Access', below) and follow the long estate track to Ben Alder Lodge
Hostel:	YHA Aviemore, Pitlochry; Independent Laggan Bridge
B&B/hotel:	Dalwhinnie
Camping:	bothy at Culra; Newtonmore; Glentruim (3km south of Newtonmore)
Access:	Ben Alder Estate, tel: 01540 672000. Walkers need permission from Network Rail to use the railway crossing at Dalwhinnie.

If you are walking in from Dalwhinnie, turn off from the main track by a metal barn at 54862 78784 and follow the path along the Allt a' Chaoil-reidhe. If you are cycling, continue past the barn on the track around the southern shores of Loch Pattack, crossing a charming little suspension bridge and heading south for 2km to another suspension bridge just before Culra Bothy is reached. Leave your bikes here and cross the bridge. Follow the path, initially along the southeast bank of the Allt a' Chaoil-reidhe. Leave this path at 51554 74446, where it begins to zigzag up the northern flanks of Beinn Bheoil. A faint trail leads through heather to the start of Ben Alder's northeast ridge, which is known as the Long Leachas. Follow the rocky ridge all the way to the top. From below, the difficulties look fairly severe, but as progress is made the problems disappear. There is a little scrambling (grade 0.5) in places, though. Towards the top the ridge narrows as the final climb is made onto the summit plateau. This stony, rounded plateau has to be crossed for 1½km to reach **Ben Alder**'s large summit cairns. The first cairn at 50039 72783 marks a minor top. Continue on to 49633 71848 to reach the trig point and main summit. Dangerous cornices tend to linger above the steep east face well into

Ben Alder from Beinn Bheoil across Loch a' Bhealaich Bheithe

summer. Take great care not to go close to this edge if snow is still present. In poor weather Ben Alder's summit can be a hard target to find (2hrs 45mins from Culra).

Continue on around the edge of the corrie to the cairn of Sron Bealach Beithe at 49928 70748, then descend the convex slope to the southeast, taking the line of least resistance over very rough ground and avoiding any rocky outcrops to reach the Bealach Breabag. From this wide col it looks as if the easiest route to Beinn Bheoil is to bypass the next hill – Sron Coire na h-Iolaire – to its left. This can be done, but it really isn't worth it. The net result is more height to climb over more difficult ground than you encounter by crossing the hill. A faint path leads from the col up to the stony summit of Sron Coire na h-Iolaire, where there is a summit cairn at 51308 70441. Traverse back to the main ridge line, and after a short drop continue quite easily to the top of **Beinn Bheoil** (51716 71712) (4hrs 15mins).

The easiest descent from here is to continue along the ridge to the north for a further 2km before dropping down easy slopes to the northwest. Cross some heather moorland to regain the path that leads back to the bridge at Culra.

ROUTE 15

Geal Charn (1132m), Carn Dearg (1034m)

Pronunciation: *Geeya Karn; Karn Jerrack*
Translation: *White Hill; Red Hill*

If you like exposed ridges, you'll enjoy the Lancet Edge. This route, which gives sensational views across the valley to Ben Alder, combines an exhilarating climb with some excellent walking between the two remote summits.

Walkers should satisfy themselves that they have the necessary permission from Network Rail to use the

Distance:	43km from Dalwhinnie (of which 27km can be cycled); 16km from Loch Pattack
Ascent:	930m from Loch Pattack
Time:	13hrs 35mins is walking fromo Dalwhinnie (5hrs less if a bike is used on estate tracks). 5hrs 35mins from Loch Pattack
Difficulty:	some simple scrambling (grade 0.5); some exposure – may become dangerous in high winds
Maps:	OS sheet 42; Explorer map 393; Area Map 1; see Route 14 for sketch map
Parking:	end of road by Dalwhinnie station, at level-crossing
Start:	cross the railway line (see 'Access', below) and along private track
Hostel:	YHA Aviemore, Pitlochry; Independent Laggan Bridge
B&B/hotel:	Dalwhinnie
Camping:	bothy at Culra; Newtonmore; Glentruim (3km south of Newtonmore)
Access:	Ben Alder Estate, tel: 01540 672000. Walkers need permission from Network Rail to use the railway crossing at Dalwhinnie

railway crossing at Dalwhinnie. (Failing this there is a bridge under the line about ½km south – turn off the A889 by a garage.) An alternative approach, which is roughly the same distance, starts from the A86 just east of Loch Laggan. An estate track can be followed from here to Loch Pattack.

Go to Loch Pattack as for Route 14. If you have cycled in from Dalwhinnie, leave your bike just south of the loch. If you have walked, follow the footpath opposite the metal barn to the suspension bridge just north of Culra. Continue on the track past Culra Bothy then follow the footpath along the northwest bank of the Allt a' Bhealaich Dhuibh until you pass beneath the first crags of Sgor Iutharn. Here take to the hillside and climb steeply up through grass and heather to gain the crest of the Lancet Edge. Continue steeply up until the ridge

Geal Charn and Sgor Iutharn from northeast ridge of Ben Alder

becomes narrow and rocky. A faint path appears and leads you through the rocks. Whilst an occasional hand is called into use on the rocks, the scrambling remains easy. However, there is a heady sensation of exposure on both sides higher up, and in a high wind this part of the ridge could become much more serious. Towards the top the ridge narrows to an arête. Although there is still no real difficulty, care does need to be taken here as there is much loose rock. At the top continue past a little cairn on the summit of Sgor Iutharn, then descend to a wide col before another short, stiff climb up the scree-spattered slope guarding **Geal Charn**'s summit plateau. In clear weather the rather pert summit cairn comes into view as soon as you get onto the plateau 46997 74617 (3hrs 35mins).

To continue to Carn Dearg cross the plateau for just over 1km to a connecting ridge that drops down sharply to a col. It may be tricky to find the right descent line here in poor visibility, but it is important to do so as there is much dangerous ground hereabouts. The only safe descent starts at 47990 75069, about 50m north of a burn that cascades down the crags. There is no path leading to this descent, but one does start quite abruptly at this grid reference and then winds quite steeply but easily down to a col. If you find yourself looking for handholds on steep rock, or sliding down very steep grass, you are definitely not on the right line. Once the col is reached the going becomes very straightforward over the little top of Diollaid a' Chairn and then up the stony summit slopes of **Carn Dearg** to the cairn at 50417 76431 (4hrs 50mins).

Descend over easy grass and heather to the north-east, dropping down to the track once the east-facing crags below Point 827 have been cleared.

DRUMOCHTER

ROUTE 16

Sgairneach Mhor (991m), Beinn Udlamain
(1011m), A' Mharconaich (975m),
Geal Charn (917m)

Pronunciation: Skarnyoch Voar;
Bine Ootlermern; Uh Varkerneach; Geeya Charn
Translation: Big Stony Hillside;
Gloomy Hill; Place of Horses; Pale Hill

Distance:	23½km
Ascent:	1050m
Time:	7hrs 15mins
Maps:	OS sheet 42; Explorer map 393; Area Map 1
Parking:	lay-by in Drumochter Pass; parking area at Balsporran Cottages
Start:	from the road cross the railway line (see 'Access', below) to join a private track
Hostel:	YHA Aviemore, Pitlochry; independent hostels Newtonmore, Laggan Bridge
B&B/hotel:	Dalwhinnie; Newtonmore; Balsporran Cottages
Camping:	Newtonmore; Glentruim (3km south of Newtonmore)
Access:	hillphone: 01528 522200 or 01796 483202. Walkers need permission from Network Rail to use the railway crossing at Dalwhinnie

The rolling hills to the west of the Drumochter Pass are a cross between the high plateau of the Cairngorms to their east and the more sharply featured ridge-lines further west. These four Munros can be climbed together to make a long but rewarding day's walk.

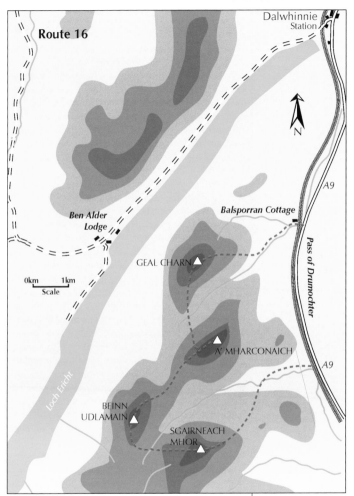

Walkers should satisfy themselves that they have the necessary permission from Network Rail to cross the railway line at the places mentioned in the route description. There are no obvious alternatives. One possibility might be to cycle in to Corrievarkie Lodge from the west end of Loch Rannoch and to climb the hills from the southwest, but this long and arduous approach would necessitate at least one night of wild camping.

Start at lay-by number 79, close to the border of Perth and Kinross and directly opposite a sign that says 'You are now at the summit of the Drumochter Pass'. For many tourists this is the highpoint of their visit to Scotland. For you the climbing has not yet begun. Happily the pass, cutting its sickle-shaped swathe through these rolling hills, gives you a great leg-up, allowing you to start this excellent circuit at an altitude of 450m.

Cross the railway line (see note above) to join a track which leads up the Allt Coire Domhain. This river must be crossed at some point, but you can stay on the track for at least 1¹/₂km before leaving it to find a path along the edge of the burn. There are many possible points to cross, but much depends on whether it is in spate. If it is, you may need to go quite a long way upstream before an easy crossing is found. Once you are over the river, climb the heather bank to the west of the col between Sgairneach Mhor and Point 758 on the OS map. At 60981 73667 turn southwest on a good path that leads up to the **Sgairneach Mhor** summit cairn and trig point 59881 73118 (2hrs).

Your next objective is the wet and boggy col between the eastern ramparts of Sgairneach Mhor and the southern spur of Beinn Udlamain. You might need to take a bearing across Sgairneach Mhor's wide, featureless, rounded top, but it is possible to travel in straight lines, first southwest for a short distance, then west to reach the col at 58335 72850. Head west from here onto the south ridge of **Beinn Udlamain**, where a line of rusty fence posts leads directly to the stony summit at 57959 73962 (3hrs 15mins).

Continue to the northeast, still following the line of fence posts. They turn abruptly to the right at one point (58375 74579) to avoid a steep, rocky slope. Reach the narrow col at 59184 75255 then continue up the southwest ridge of **A' Mharconaich**. It is some 2km to the summit cairn, which is right at the far end of the plateau at 60484 76339 (4hrs 30mins).

Once again, finding the right line to the next hill can be tricky in poor weather. Retrace your steps for about 1km to 59929 75863, then head northwest down grassy slopes, avoiding small crags at the bottom of the slope on the left, to 59398 76266. At this point head directly to the col at 59256 76623. From here it is a straightforward climb up the southern slopes of Geal Charn (there are four Munros of this name within a few miles of here and no fewer than 19 tops in all sharing this name). Climb up to the summit on the east side of the broad ridge – don't be seduced by the track that leads back along the valley from here to Balsporran Cottages. Climb to **Geal Charn**'s stony round summit. There are actually two cairns at the top separated by about 100m (59649 78282) (5hrs 40mins).

From the top a heavily eroded path leads easily down the broad northeast spur through heather and peat to Balsporran Cottages and the A9.

ROUTE 17

Meall Chuaich (951m)

Pronunciation: Miaowl Chu-weech
Translation: Hill of the Bowl or Quaich

Distance:	14km
Ascent:	610m
Time:	4hrs
Maps:	OS sheet 42; Explorer map 394; Area Map 2
Parking:	Lay-by 94 on the A9
Start:	along a private track off the A9
Hostel:	YHA Aviemore, Pitlochry; independent hostels Newtonmore, Laggan Bridge
B&B/hotel:	Dalwhinnie; Newtonmore; Kingussie
Camping:	Newtonmore; Glentruim (3km south of Newtonmore)
Access:	Cuaich Estate, tel: 01540 673568

WALKING THE MUNROS – SOUTHERN, CENTRAL AND WESTERN HIGHLANDS

Lying to the east of Dalwhinnie and the A9, this hill stands somewhat apart from the main plateau and makes for a relatively short but pleasant walk.

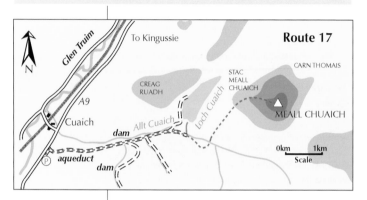

From lay-by number 79 on the A9, pass through the gate just south of Cuaich and take to a private track. This track immediately joins another one and heads up the valley of the Allt Cuaich, passing alongside an aqueduct. Stay on the track when it crosses the aqueduct to reach the Cuaich power station. Pass this, then cross a little bridge and take the left fork when the track branches. Cross another little bridge and immediately take a left fork again. When the loch is clearly in sight, but about 200m before you reach it, take a right fork. This leads past a little bothy (currently locked). Continue for about ½km, crossing a bridge over the Allt Coire Chuaich, before leaving the track and striking out northeast up the steep heathery hillside. An eroded path leads up onto the western shoulder of Meall Chuaich. From the flat of the shoulder turn east and climb over stony ground to the huge summit cairn at 71645 87820 (2hrs 30mins).

Return by the same route.

ROUTE 18

A' Bhuidheanach Bheag (936m),

Carn na Caim (941m)

Pronunciation: *Uh Vooyernoch Vayk; Karn na Kyme*
Translation: *The Little Yellow Hill; Cairn of the Curve*

Distance:	18km
Ascent:	890m
Time:	5hrs 30mins
Difficulty:	navigation can be very tricky in poor visibility on this feature less plateau
Maps:	OS sheet 42; Explorer map 394; Area Map 2
Parking:	lay-by 88 on the A9 just south of the Dalwhinnie turn-off
Start:	along private track just south of the lay-by
Hostel:	YHA Aviemore, Pitlochry; Independent Laggan Bridge, Newtonmore
B&B/hotel:	Dalwhinnie; Newtonmore
Camping:	Newtonmore; Glentruim (3km south of Newtonmore)
Access:	Drumochter Estate, tel: 01528 522291

To the east of the Drumochter Pass lies a range of rounded hills fringed by a series of deep, heathery corries. On top of the range is an extensive undulating plateau, which can offer a real test of navigational skills in poor weather. The two Munros in the range are fairly undistinguished hills, which are easily accessed from the A9.

The easiest way onto the plateau is via a quarryman's track that starts just south of Lay-by 88. There is a healthy population of mountain hares living on the plateau, as indeed there is on the other side of the Drumochter Pass. Many of these hares have been fitted with radio collars, and their movements and life-cycles carefully monitored

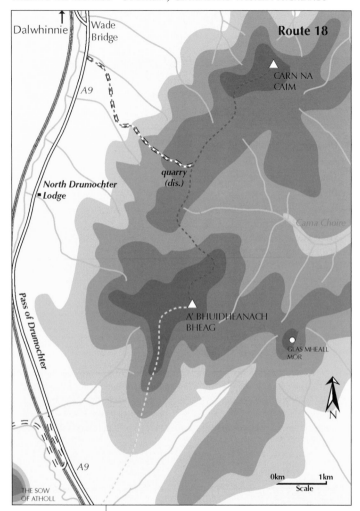

Route 18

Dalwhinnie

Wade Bridge

A9

CARN NA CAIM

North Drumochter
■ Lodge

quarry (dis.)

Cama Choire

A' BHUIDHEANACH BHEAG

Pass of Drumochter

GLAS MHEALL MOR

A9

THE SOW OF ATHOLL

0km   1km
Scale

N

over the years. Follow the track all the way up onto a little cairned top, Point 902. Regrettably this track has been extended so that a Landrover trail now runs north and

*The western flanks
of A' Bhuidheanach
Bheag*

south over much of the plateau. Head for a low cairned hill – A' Bhuidheanach (Point 879) – which hardly looks like a hill at all from Point 902. Then cross a peaty col before climbing gently up to the cairned summit of **A' Bhuidheanach Bheag** 66075 77600 (2hrs 50mins).

A fairly direct line can be taken on to Carn na Caim, but the easiest way is to return by the route of ascent to Point 902, then cross another small hill (Point 914) before dropping and rising again to **Carn na Caim** 67685 82110 (4hrs 10mins).

Return by the route of ascent.

ATHOLL

ROUTE 19

Beinn Dearg (1008m)

Pronunciation: *Bine Jerrack*
Translation: *Red Hill*

Beinn Dearg is a remote, dome-shaped granite hill set in some fairly bleak moorland on the southern edge of the high Mounth plateau. Being somewhat distant from neighbouring Munros it is climbed alone and is usually approached from Glen Banvie, starting near the Old Bridge of Tilt.

There is a track that goes from Calvine on the A9 along Glen Bruar to the old Bruar Lodge, and the hill can be climbed from here after crossing the river at Bruar Lodge. However it is more usually climbed via a track from Old Blair, as described here.

Distance:	28km (of which some 19km can be cycled)
Ascent:	930m
Time:	7hrs 55mins (2hrs 15mins less if a bike is used)
Maps:	OS sheet 43; Explorer map 394 and 386; Area Map 2
Parking:	car park near Old Bridge of Tilt
Start:	along public road that skirts to the north of Old Blair, then private estate track
Hostel:	YHA Pitlochry; Independent Pitlochry
B&B/hotel:	Blair Atholl, Pitlochry
Camping:	Faskally; Blair Atholl; Struan
Access:	Atholl Estate, tel: hillphone 01796 481740 or 01796 481355

From the car park near the Old Bridge of Tilt, take the road to Old Blair, but turn right before this small village is reached. At the next junction cross over to join a private track and follow this through trees on the north side of the river. This track can be quite muddy in places at first. Cross a stile and continue on the track for some way up the little valley of the Allt na Moine Baine before it then heads over a fairly desolate stretch of moorland to reach the remote Snaicheachan Bothy, about 6km from Beinn Dearg. This track can be cycled all the way, though it is steep in places and quite rough. From the bothy a very rough track continues up the Allt Snaicheachan before it doubles back onto the flanks of Beinn a' Chait. A path leads off from this track up the southern ridge of Beinn Dearg. Once the first nose is climbed, cross a short section of wet heather moorland then climb steadily on good ground, passing a small cairned minor top before the red granite stones of **Beinn Dearg**'s summit are

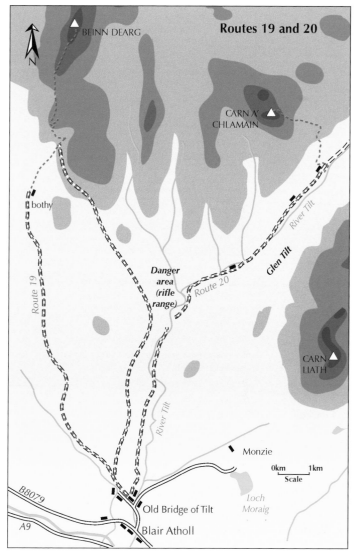

Routes 19 and 20

BEINN DEARG

CARN A' CHLAMAIN

bothy

Route 19

River Tilt

Glen Tilt

Danger area (rifle range)

Route 20

CARN LIATH

River Tilt

Monzie

0km 1km
Scale

B8079

A9

Old Bridge of Tilt

Blair Atholl

Loch Moraig

N

reached. The summit cairn is at 85291 77772 (4hrs 45mins; less if a bike is used).

Return by the route of ascent to the track. For variety this track can be followed for a short distance up Beinn a' Chait before a bulldozed track (not currently marked on the OS map) leads easily back along the Allt Slanaidh to Old Blair.

ROUTE 20

Carn a' Chlamain (963m)

Pronunciation: Karn uh Chlaveen
Translation: Hill of the Kite

Distance:	31km (of which 23km can be cycled)
Ascent:	660m
Time:	9hrs 25mins (about 3hrs 40mins can be saved if using a bike on the estate track)
Maps:	OS sheet 43; Explorer map 394 and 386; Area Map 2; see Route 19 for sketch map
Parking:	the Glen Tilt car park, 1 mile north of Blair Atholl
Start:	along a private track that starts opposite the car park signposted to Glen Tilt.
Hostel:	YHA Pitlochry; Independent Pitlochry
B&B/hotel:	Blair Atholl, Pitlochry
Camping:	Faskally; Blair Atholl; Struan
Access:	hillphone: 01796 481740 or 01796 481355. The Atholl Estate also runs a visitor information room in Blair Atholl in the summer months.

This distant hill is most easily accessed by bike via the lovely Tilt Valley. It makes a popular and pleasant objective.

The days when you could drive up Glen Tilt to the foot of Carn a' Chlamain and pop up it before breakfast are long-since gone. The Atholl Estate, following the recommendation of the Cairngorm Working Party, have sensibly closed Glen Tilt to motorised vehicles (at least to those of the general public). The resulting 11½km walk-in to Forest Lodge has restored some of the remoteness and the 'wilderness feel' to this beautiful area. If you prefer it you can, of course, cycle to Forest Lodge along the excellent track and leave your bike in the wood before taking to the hill.

On leaving the car park, cross the road and take the track that starts at the gates to the right of the house. The track follows the River Tilt, first on one side then the other; sometimes far above it, sometimes alongside. The mixed woodland and pretty scenery have made this into a popular walk in its own right. Follow the track, making sure you avoid the firing range to the west (red flags are displayed when this is in use) until the valley narrows into a deeply incised U-shaped glacial valley. There is much to see of interest along this beautiful valley, but if you're cycling be warned by an upturned car in the River Tilt above Marble Lodge – it pays to stop first if you're going to gaze at the wildlife.

There is a rather ugly, recently bulldozed track up the southeast ridge of the hill over Gaire Clach-Ghlais, but a much pleasanter way onto the hill is to continue to Forest Lodge. Pass the lodge and go on to the end of the wood, where the road is gated. Leave bikes here and go through the gate, then turn back along the edge of the wood until a path climbs steeply up the hillside. The path zigzags its way above the valley until it reaches a peat and heather moorland above. From here the well-beaten trail continues for 2km onto a broad ridge before it passes within a midge's whisker of the summit of **Carn a' Chlamain**. At 91671 75867 turn southwest and make the short stony climb to the summit cairn at 91595 75798 (2hrs 15mins from Forest Lodge).

Return by the same route.

BEINN A' GHLO

(Hooded Mountain)

ROUTE 21

Carn Liath (975m),
Braigh Coire Chruinn-bhalgain (1070m),
Carn nan Gabhar (1129m)

Pronunciation: *Karn Leeya; Bry Korrer Chrain Valler-ghen; Karn ner Goer*
Translation: *Grey Hill; Height of the Corrie of Round Blisters; Hill of Goats*

Distance:	21km
Ascent:	1300m
Time:	7hrs 10mins
Maps:	OS sheet 43; Explorer maps 394 and 386; Area Map 2
Parking:	roadside by Loch Moraig near Monzie
Start:	along private track signposted to Shinagag
Hostel:	YHA Pitlochry; Independent Pitlochry
B&B/hotel:	Blair Atholl; Pitlochry
Camping:	Faskally; Blair Atholl; Struan
Access:	Atholl, tel: hillphone 01796 481355; Lude Steading, tel: 01796 481460

The three Munros to the east of Glen Tilt form the highest points of the Forest of Atholl and make a good circuit, offering pleasant walking and plenty of interest. Very little time or energy is saved by doing just one or two of these Munros. They are invariably approached from Monzie to the southwest, although they can be reached from Glen Tilt itself or from Glen Fearnach to the east, though with rather more effort.

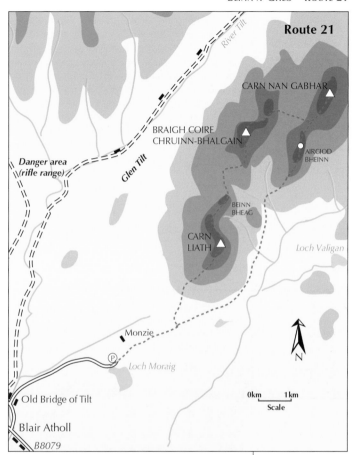

Cars can be parked at the north end of Loch Moraig. From here go through the gate signposted to Shinagag and follow the private track as far as two wooden huts. At this point leave the track and head north-northeast to join an obvious eroded path that takes the easiest line up **Carn Liath**. A cairn high up on the shoulder leads on a little higher to another cairn at the summit (93608 69824) (2hrs 10mins).

From here, the ridge to Braigh Coire Chruinn-bhalgain snakes away alternately to the northwest and northeast. It is an easy ridge to follow and gives pleasant walking. Quite a lot of height is lost dropping to the narrow col below Braigh Coire Chuinn-bhalgain. (There is an easy descent route from this col if required: a good path winds down between Beinn Mhaol and Beinn Bheag, crosses the little burn and skirts around the south-eastern flank of Carn Liath to rejoin the Shinagag track.) From the col climb the curving ridge to the summit of **Braigh Coire Chruinn-bhalgain** staying close to the crest all the way (94563 72402) (3hrs 30mins).

The path continues to snake, this time northeast and east, as it drops to another col beneath **Carn nan Gabhar**. Climb the easy slope on the other side of the col, then head northeast along the long stony summit ridge. The path disappears amongst all the stones on this broad ridge but there are three large markers to head for in poor weather. First a large cairn on a huge pile of stones is passed. Next comes a trig point, which is also passed. Finally, a couple of hundred metres beyond the trig point, is another large cairn marking the highest point on the ridge at 97126 73302 (4hrs 40mins).

The best way down is to retrace your steps along the summit ridge and then continue over Airgiod Bheinn.

Beinn a' Ghlo – Carn na Gabhar from Aigiod Bheinn

102

This is another very stony ridge, narrower than the last, but with a path along the crest that is easy to follow. The most straightforward descent is to continue along the length of the ridge and drop down over the southwestern nose of the hill, where the angle of descent is shallowest. The path descends through a little valley that is hardly discernable on the 1:50,000 map, then crosses heather to reach the Allt Bealach an Fhiodha. Just beyond this burn a more prominent path takes you back to the Shinagag track. This path divides after about 1km, but both branches will take you back to the track about 1½km from the two wooden huts. From here it is an easy walk of 3½km back to Loch Moraig.

GLEN SHEE

ROUTE 22

Glas Tulaichean (1051m),
Carn an Righ (1029m)

Pronunciation: *Glaz Toolachein; Karn ern Ree*
Translation: *Grey-green Knoll; Cairn of the King*

Distance:	25km
Ascent:	970m
Time:	7hrs 20mins from Dalmunzie House Hotel
Maps:	OS sheet 43; Explorer map 387; Area Map 2
Parking:	Dalmunzie House Hotel
Start:	along estate track through Glenlochsie Farm
Hostel:	YHA Braemar; Independent Spittal of Glenshee
B&B/hotel:	Spittal of Glenshee
Camping:	Braemar
Access:	Dalmunzie, tel: 01250 885226

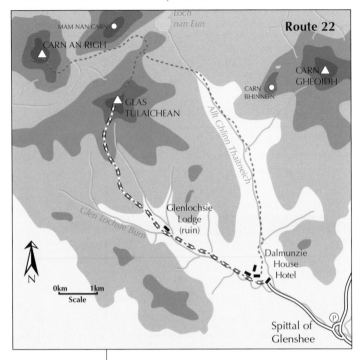

Route 22

At the southern end of the great Cairngorm massif, a number of deeply cut glens slice into the plateau, giving access to the walker on this side of the range. Glen Lochsie and Glen Taitneach, to the south and east of Glas Tulaichean respectively, make the start and finish lines of a good long circuit that can also incorporate Carn an Righ. Although one or both of these hills could be included in a very long day from Glen Ey, they are much more usually climbed from the south.

Park at the Spittal of Glen Shee, or in the designated area not far inside the grounds of the Dalmunzie House Hotel, or, if you prefer it, 2km further on at the hotel itself, where a small charge will be levied (currently £2). Continue on the track past Glenlochsie Farm, but before this track fords the Glen Lochsie Burn, leave it to join a path that follows the line of the old railway on the north side of the burn. If you stay on the Landrover track you will have to cross the burn again higher up, only this time with rather more difficulty. Once the ruins of Glenlochsie Lodge are reached, the climbing begins up one of the long southern ridges of Glas Tulaichean. The Landrover track makes the going very easy, although it is steep at first. At the highest point of the track, just before it begins to lose height, a short walk over grass brings you to the summit of **Glas Tulaichean**, where there is a trig point at 05104 76001 (3hrs from the hotel).

Descend the northeast ridge for ½km, then veer round to the north over Point 930 to arrive at the col above Glas Choire Bheag. The watery quagmire to your left now has to be crossed, but if you continue part-way round the little hill in front of you (Point 858) and cross to the northeast of the bog, very little difficulty should be encountered. Once across, traverse west below the steep flanks of Mam nan Carn, where a good path appears. Follow this to the western nose of this hill, where the path crosses a small col and begins to climb onto the southern ridge of **Carn an Righ**. Once on the ridge the going is quite easy over short grass interspersed with scree. At the top there is a more extensive blanket of stones. The summit cairn is at 02872 77255 (4hrs 40mins from the hotel).

Return by the route of ascent as far as the col above Glas Choire Bheag, then descend east into this corrie. The exact line is not important, although the easiest way through the peat hags is probably on the north side of the corrie. Cross the Allt Easgaidh at the bottom and follow the path, then the track, for several kilometres along Glean Taitneach. Some ancient archaeology has been found in this long, glaciated valley, including very old settlements and some field systems on both sides of the valley that extend quite a long way up it. About 1km from Glenlochsie Farm, a wooden bridge allows you to cross the river and rejoin the track between the farm and Dalmunzie House Hotel. Staying on the east side of the river will bring you out at the Spittal of Glenshee.

ROUTE 23

*Creag Leacach (987m), Glas
Maol (1068m), Cairn of Claise
(1064m), Tom Buidhe (957m),
Tolmount (958m), Carn an Tuirc (1019m)*

*Pronunciation: Krayk Lairkoch; Glaz Merle; Karn
uh Clash; Tom Booyer; Tolmount; Karn ern Toork*
*Translation: Crag of the Bare Hilltop;
The Grey-green Bald Head; Cairn of the Hollow;
Yellow Knoll; Hollow of the Mounth; Hill of the Boar*

Distance:	22km
Ascent:	1120m
Time:	7hrs 15mins (plus 1 hour if walking the road between the two car parks)
Maps:	OS sheets 43 and 44; Explorer maps 387 and 388; Harvey's Superwalker map Lochnagar and Glenshee; Area Map 2
Parking:	lay-by on A93 to NW of Leacach at 13956 75670
Start:	from lay-by straight onto hill
Hostel:	YHA Braemar; Independent Glenshee
B&B/hotel:	Braemar
Camping:	Braemar
Access:	Leacach and Glas Maol, hillphone: 01250 885288. Cairn of Claise, Tolmount and Carn an Tuirc, hillphone: 013397 41997. Tom Buidhe, hillphone: 01575 550335

These hills can be tackled in various combinations from the Glenshee Ski Centre at the top of the pass, but the walk described here is far more satisfying. It is well away from the ski lifts and fences and offers a fine mountain circuit across the southern Cairngorms with a rare chance to cover six Munros quite comfortably in one outing.

The A93 climbs through Glen Shee and Gleann Beag past the Glenshee Ski Centre before dropping gradually down to Braemar. From the hillwalker's point of view, the group of six Munros to the east of the ski centre is far less affected by tow bars and other skiing development than might be supposed. This walk starts at the lay-by at 13956 75670, but many parties leave a car at 14752 80002, where the walk ends, and take a bike or second car to the starting-point to save the 5km walk along the road at the end of the day. The hills here are formed of granite intrusions through quartz and schist and they have been heavily incised by glacial valleys. Look out for the beautiful dwarf cornel in summer months, along with cloudberry, bog bearberry and, on higher ground, the trailing azalea growing on the acidic soil.

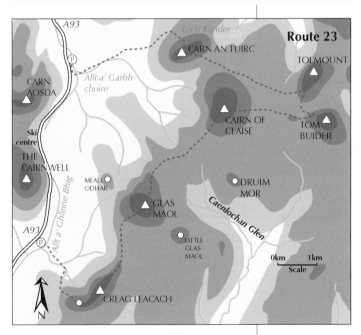

From the lay-by, descend to the Allt a' Ghlinne Bhig, which you cross, then proceed along the north side of the burn that flows down from Creag Leacach. After 1km cross this burn and head south up a grassy slope to the col between Meall Gorm and the southwestern outlier of Creag Leacach (Point 943 on the OS map). Towards the top of the col veer round to reach the stony mantle of quartzite that covers most of this hill, reaching the outlier at 14776 74246. From here climb the curving ridge, following a stone wall, to **Creag Leacach**'s summit cairn, which is actually set into the wall at 15472 74538 (1hr 35mins).

Continue along the stony undulating ridge for 1½km, staying close to the wall and picking your way through the shattered quartzite rocks and scree that cover this hill. A cairn at the end of the wall (16011 75870) marks the point where you change direction to the northeast, climbing the grassy slopes of **Glas Maol** to the large summit cairn capping its rounded dome (16702 76567) (2hrs 25mins).

There is an easy descent to the ski centre from here, but to continue, drop down the northern slopes of Glas Maol, picking up the line of an old drover's road – the

Looking up to Carn an Tuirc from the Allt a' Gharb Coire

Monega road. Cross a broad, peat-covered col before veering right (east) around the head of the Garbh Choire. From here you turn to the northeast, passing a small lochan, to reach the stony slopes that lead to the summit cairn of **Cairn of Claise** (18550 78881) (3hrs 30mins).

This is a good vantage point for taking in the great plateau of the Mounth spread out before you. Viewed from here Tom Buidhe – your next objective – is little more than a small bump in the huge landscape to the east. It actually looks smaller than much of the surrounding countryside. The absence of obvious features in the landscape also makes it look closer than it is. In poor weather it can be a difficult target to find. From Cairn of Claise head east for 3km, crossing peaty, wet ground and skirting Ca Whims – which is little more than a rough patch on the gentle slopes of **Tom Buidhe** – to reach the summit at 21367 78766 (4hrs 20mins).

Descend to the north of Ca Whims, skirting round the head of the corrie that cuts between Tom Buidhe and Tolmount, then head north to reach the summit cairn of **Tolmount** at 21051 80005 (5hrs).

Retrace your steps for a short distance, then head southwest to grid reference 20544 79452 in order to avoid the steep-sided corrie – Glen Callater – to your north. From here you can reset your compass to a west-northwest course, taking you on a long traverse of the hillside to the broad saddle between Cairn of Claise and Carn an Tuirc. Once on the saddle, climb the stony slopes of **Carn an Tuirc**, your last hill of the day. The first cairn you reach, to the east of the broad summit ridge at 17806 80539, is not as high as its neighbour a few hundred metres away. Cross the broad, level, stony ridge to reach the higher cairn at 17424 80462 (6hrs 20mins).

To descend, go back to a slight depression in the middle of the ridge and head north. In poor weather, don't descend before reaching 17506 80784. The slope drops quite steeply at first, then more gently to reach an old, ruined wooden hut, of which there is now very little left. From here a path winds back through the heather to a little bridge over the Allt a' Gharbh-choire and so to the car park.

ROUTE 24

Carn a' Gheoidh (975m),

The Cairnwell (933m),

Carn Aosda (917m)

Pronunciation: *Karn uh Yoye; the Cairnwell; Carn Ooster*
Translation: *Hill of the Goose; Hill of Bags; Aged Hill*

Distance:	13km
Ascent:	580m
Time:	4hrs
Maps:	OS sheet 43; Explorer map 387; Harvey's Superwalker map Lochnagar and Glenshee; Area Map 2
Parking:	ski centre car park at the summit of the pass
Start:	from ski centre climb up bulldozed ski track and straight onto the hill
Hostel:	YHA Braemar; Independent Glenshee
B&B/hotel:	Braemar; Spittal of Glenshee
Camping:	Braemar
Access:	hillphone: 01250 885288

The three Munros that have been most affected by the Glenshee ski development, on the west side of the pass, can be reached with less height climbed than any other Munro, largely because they sit so close to the road and are just above the highest point of the pass. The car can be parked at an altitude of 675m, leaving just a hop and a skip to the first summit and the chance to do three Munros with very little effort.

From the car park at the ski centre, go to the far right-hand end of all the buildings and head west up the heathery slopes to the col, avoiding the bulldozed track which you cross halfway up. Round the last fence at the

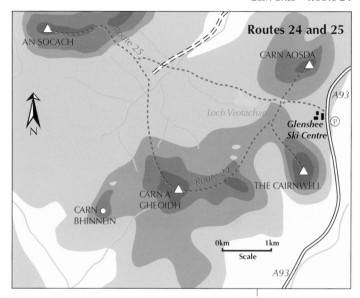

Routes 24 and 25

AN SOCACH

Route 25

CARN AOSDA

A93

N

Loch Vrotachan

Glenshee Ski Centre Ⓟ

Route 24

THE CAIRNWELL

CARN A' GHEOIDH

CARN BHINNEIN

0km   1km
Scale

A93

Much has been written about the despoliation of the hills by the ski industry here, but the proximity of Carn Aosda and The Cairnwell to the car park would always have made them 'tourist routes', and the fact remains that within 20mins of the car park you can lose sight altogether of the tow bars and other ski paraphernalia. The walk to Carn a' Gheoidh and back is a surprisingly pleasant one in a wild and beautiful landscape.

top and before you reach Loch Vrotachan pick up the path that skirts around the steep corrie between The Cairnwell and Carn nan Sac. Continue pleasantly along the ridge in a southwesterly direction, passing two small lochans and taking a small diversion if you wish to the summit of Carn nan Sac. The ridge then turns to the west and broadens to become a fairly flat promontory before a final little climb brings you to the cairn on the summit dome of **Carn a' Gheoidh** at 10701 76683 (1hr 40mins).

Carn a' Gheoidh from the slopes of An Socach

Return by the same route, passing over the lump to the north of Carn nan Sac with the fine prospect of the Cairnwell's baggy ridge (hence 'hill of bags') and its steep west flank before you. Start the climb onto this ridge at 12721 78135. Soon you reach the line of fences and the ski tow, then a short steep step leads to **Cairnwell**'s summit cairn, which is squeezed rather meanly between two radio masts at 13486 77350 (2hrs 50mins).

Descend to the col, and another short climb to the northeast brings you to the summit of **Carn Aosda** (13388 79137) (3hrs 30mins).

Pick your route back to the car park.

ROUTE 25

An Socach (944m)

Pronunciation: *Un Sorcoch*
Translation: *The Snout*

Climb up from the ski centre to the col and pass to the north of Loch Vrotachan, crossing the heather and peat moorland that drops down eventually to the Baddoch

Distance:	14km
Ascent:	790m
Time:	4hrs 10mins
Maps:	OS sheet 43; Explorer map 387; Harvey's Superwalker map Lochnagar and Glenshee; see Route 24 for sketch map
Parking:	the ski centre car park
Start:	up bulldozed ski track
Hostel:	Braemar
B&B/hotel:	Braemar
Camping:	Braemar
Access:	Invercauld Estate, tel: 013397 41224

An Socach is a long, stony, humpback ridge that lies well concealed by other hills from any road. It is usually climbed on its own either from Baddoch or from the ski centre on the A93. However it can easily be included in the Route 24 to make a more interesting circuit.

The approach from Baddoch is along a bulldozed private track. Cars cannot be taken along here, but a bike could take you right to the base of the hill (although the last kilometre may be a little steep). The approach from the ski centre is rather more interesting once the col is reached above the ski slopes.

Burn. This burn can be quite full at times, but there are plenty of stones offering possible crossing places. Once across, head for the obvious gap between the west and east summits of **An Socach**, crossing heather slopes to reach it. Climb up on the right (east) side of the little burn that comes down from the col. At the top, turn left onto the long, stony summit ridge and walk to its western end, where a cairn and a stone enclosure a few metres apart mark the highest point at 07981 79968 (2hrs 20mins).

If you are including An Socach with the previous route, head down the long north-northwest ridge from Carn a' Gheoidh to cross the Baddoch Burn higher up, then continue to the gap on An Socach's long ridge, climb it and return by the route described above.

THE LOCHNAGAR HILLS

ROUTE 26
Cac Carn Beag (1155m),
Carn a' Choire Bhaidheach (1110m),
Carn an t-Sagairt Mor (1047m),
Cairn Bannoch (1012m),
Broad Cairn (998m)

Pronunciation: *Kac Karn Bayk; Karn uh Korrer Vaw-yeech;*
Karn ern Taggert More; Cairn Bannoch; Broad Cairn
Translation: *Slope of the Wee Cairn; Cairn of*
the Beautiful Corrie; Big Hill of the Priest; Hill of the Point

Lochnagar is one of the jewels of the southern Cairngorms, beloved by walkers and climbers alike, and the round of the five Munros described here makes for a wonderful outing at any time of the year. This route can be split to make two or three outings, but since all of the hard work is in getting onto the plateau, most parties will want to stay high once they're up and do the lot in one outing. This makes for an excellent day's walk, and although quite a long distance has to be covered there is not a great deal of climbing involved after the first summit and the going is mostly very easy.

From the car park in the Spittal of Glenmuick, walk past the visitor centre and take the track that leads over the River Muick and across a stretch of flat land to the buildings at Allt na-giubhsaich. The track bypasses the buildings here, then passes through a wood of fine Scots

Distance:	28km
Ascent:	1260m
Time:	9hrs
Maps:	OS sheet 44; Explorer map 388; Harvey's Superwalker map Lochnagar and Glenshee; Area Map 2
Parking:	car park at the Spittal of Glenmuick (small charge – take coins for machine)
Start:	along estate track past visitor centre
Hostel:	Ballater
B&B/hotel:	Ballater
Camping:	Ballater
Access:	hillphone: 01575 550335 or 013397 42534; visitor centre, tel: 013397 55059. Details of local stalking may be posted in the visitor centre during key times such as the stag hunting season.

To the southwest of Ballater the River Muick has cut a broad valley, much loved by deer and other wildlife, deep into the White Mounth. The whole route described here falls within the royal estate of Balmoral. Queen Victoria walked here, and Prince Charles wrote a story about the Old Man of Lochnagar. These days you are quite likely to see an old man on Lochnagar. And an old woman too. And come to that all manner of other folk, as these hills are extremely popular. Often the car park is full to over-flowing in summer.

Where there are paths on these hills, they tend to be more visible than in many other areas. Many of the estate tracks have been bulldozed, leaving ugly scars, but even on the tops the pressure of many feet has taken its toll, especially on Lochnagar itself, where the granite seems to be exceptionally friable and easily eroded.

pines with a blaeberry ground-cover before emerging onto the open hillside. Stay on the track as it winds around the hillside, gradually gaining height, until about 3km from Allt na-giubgsaich an obvious path leads off to the left. Descend briefly along this path, then begin the

115

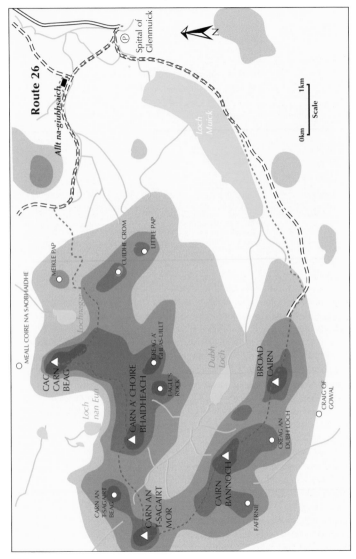

gradual climb up to the col at 25789 85783 between Meikle Pap and the dramatic cirque above the loch (2hrs 25mins).

Once on the col the path steepens over a section known as the Ladder, where it winds its way between large granite blocks to emerge at 25651 85298. The steep path on the Ladder was once 'improved' to assist Queen Victoria in her ascent of Lochnagar. Above the Ladder the main path stays well back from the edge of the cirque (which can become heavily corniced in places in winter), but climbs easily to the huge summit cairn of Cac Carn Mor, perched impressively on top of a small granite tor at 24509 85680. It's just a few hundred metres on to the summit rocks and cairn of **Cac Carn Beag** at 24371 86128. From here there are fine views across the Balmoral Forest to the northern Caingorms. There are good views also to your next objective – Carn a' Choire Bhaidheach (sometimes spelt Bhoidhich) – across the Loch nan Eun and its cohort of cliffs (3hrs 30mins to the summit of Cac Carn Beag).

Retrace your steps to just below the summit of Cac Carn Mor, where the path splits into two. Taking the right-hand path head down towards the top rim of the cliffs that enclose Loch nan Eun. Continue around the head of

Looking north from summit of Cac Carn Beag

Carn a' Choire Bhaidheach and Loch nan Eun from Cac Carn Beag

this corrie until at 23081 84908 you leave the path and head southwest up wind-clipped grassy slopes to the summit of **Carn a' Choire Bhaidheach** 22671 84548 (4hrs 20mins).

Drop down to the northwest to regain the path. Quite a bit of height has to be lost here. The path continues across the infant Allt an Dubh-loch, skirting around the minor top – Carn an t-Sagairt Beag – and then around the base of the next Munro: **Carn an t-Sagairt Mor**. Leave the path to clamber up the southeastern slopes of this hill, where large granite blocks are sunk into a bed of moss and wind-blown heath. The summit cairn is at 20749 84406 (5hrs 10mins).

On a clear day there is a good view from Carn an t-Sagairt Mor of the knobbly granite top of your next hill, Cairn Bannoch. Drop down to the south-southeast, crossing the path you were on before, to reach a peaty mire on the broad saddle between Carn an t-Sagairt Mor and Fafernie. The path from here is hard to lose unless it's under snow, etched as it is into the fragile granite slope. Climb gently onto the flanks of Fafernie, then turn south-east and, with very little additional climbing, reach the rocky knob that is the summit of **Cairn Bannoch** at 22288 82549 (5hrs 45mins).

Continue southeast over an unnamed minor top, at 991m on the OS map, then bypass the Cairn of Gowal, veering east-southeast to cross a wide col until the slope steepens and becomes strewn with rounded granite blocks all the way to the summit of **Broad Cairn** at 24054 81557 (6hrs 25mins).

From this top the path winds eastwards, dropping rapidly over a jumble of boulders until it meets a stony bulldozed track which has been cut aggressively across this fragile landscape. About 2km from the summit, pass a tin hut used by stalkers, and shortly after this two small cairns mark the start of the footpath off to the left which finds a way through the heather and down into Corrie Chash to reach the shores of Loch Muick. It is a lovely walk along the loch back to the car park, although many summer tourists come this way, which is sadly reflected in the quantities of sweet papers, tissues and other litter that can collect here despite the efforts of estate workers.

Walk the full length of the loch, passing another group of Scots pines, before returning to the visitor centre and car park.

GLEN CLOVA

ROUTE 27
Mayar (928m), Driesh (947m)

Pronunciation: Mayer; Dreesh
Translation: High Plain; The Bramble

As you travel up the long valley of Glen Clova, with its beautiful high corries and hanging valleys, the hills on either side gradually become higher and more enclosing until, at its far northwestern end, the glen slices deep into the southern heartland of the Mounth. The pair of much frequented Munros that lie to the south of the Glendoll Forest no doubt owe some of their popularity to their ease of access from the cities of the south, but they also offer a good taste of the wild plateau formation of the Mounth and make for a very pleasant excursion, with excellent views across a wide area including the hills of Lochnagar and Glenshee and a glimpse of the North Sea.

Distance:	14km
Ascent:	860m
Time:	4hrs 30mins
Maps:	OS sheet 44; Explorer map 388; Harvey's Superwalker map Lochnagar and Glenshee; Area Map 2
Parking:	car park at the end of Glen Doll
Start:	along forestry track below the youth hostel
Hostel:	the youth hostel in Glen Doll is now closed, as is Perth YHA which used to be the next nearest. There is now no youth hostel within reasonable reach of this area.
B&B/hotel:	Clova; Kirriemuir
Camping:	Glen Clova campsite is closed at the time of writing and looks unlikely to reopen
Access:	Airlie Estate, tel: 01575 550230

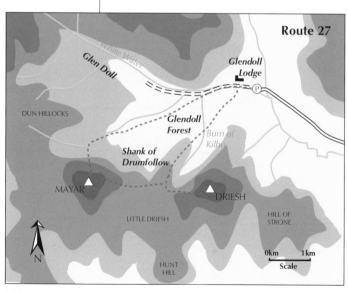

From the car park take the track past a farm below the former hostel (there's no need to take the track up to the building itself). Cross the bridge over the White Water and continue on for about 100m to reach a gate in the track. Take the forest trail to the right of the main track. Follow this through the trees for 1½km, staying close to the White Water. Note the path that leads off to the left after 250m – this is your descent path back from Driesh. Soon the trail splits into two. One way takes you across a bridge over the river – ignore this and instead take the left fork that leads up through trees. Ignore a turning off to the right higher up. The track eventually narrows into a path before it passes through a gate to emerge from the trees into a high cwm, a superb rock-strewn amphitheatre drained by the Fee Burn.

Cross the flat pasture then climb steeply up the back of the cwm, passing to the left of an attractive little waterfall. A path can be followed right to the top where the angle eventually eases off, but higher up the path becomes less distinct. In ascent there is no difficulty; if descending this way, however, it may be difficult to pick up the correct line of the descent path.

At grid reference 24146 74628 leave the path and head south over grassy, windswept slopes to reach the summit of **Mayar** at 24032 73748. There are fine views from here on a clear day across the southern Cairngorms (2hrs 30mins).

From here head east on a well-trodden trail across a flattish section for nearly 2km to the Shank of Drumfollow. Drop down to a small col between here and Little Driesh, then ascend across the flanks of Little Driesh and on to **Driesh** itself, where there is a trig point inside the summit stone enclosure (27125 73603) (3hrs 30mins).

To descend, retrace your steps to the col below Little Driesh and climb a short distance onto the Shank of Drumfollow to join a substantial path (cairned at the very top). This hugs the side of the ridge to the west of the Burn of Kilbo until it passes through a gate and enters the Glendoll Forest. The path drops rapidly through the forest, crossing a couple of forestry tracks lower down until it rejoins the trail along the White Water. Turn right along this trail and follow the outward route back to the car park.

GLEN ESK

ROUTE 28
Mount Keen (939m)

Pronunciation: Mount Keen
Translation: Gentle Hill

Distance:	18km
Ascent:	680m
Time:	4hrs 30mins
Maps:	OS sheet 44; Explorer map 395; Area Map 2
Parking:	car park at Invermark
Start:	footpath to Glen Mark
Hostel:	YHA Perth is probably the nearest if approaching from the south; Ballater is closer if approaching from the north
B&B/hotel:	Glen Esk
Camping:	southeastern end of Glen Esk
Access:	Dalhousie Estate, tel: 01356 670208

Far to the east of all the other Munros, Mount Keen sits in splendid isolation at the head of Glen Mark.

From the car park in Invermark at the head of Glen Esk, continue for a short distance along the road and take the first right turn, which is signposted to the Queen's Well. A grassy lane leads to the left of a house, passing through

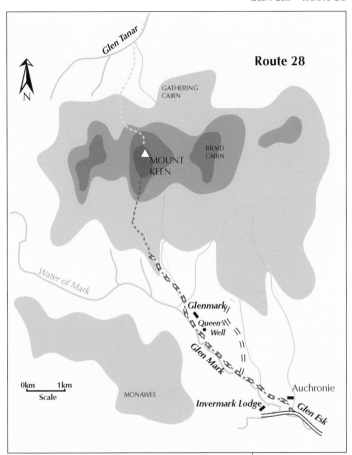

two gates. The second of these is a battered but rather fine old iron one, which may well date from the time of Queen Victoria, who once visited this valley. The stony path is obvious. Ignore a turning to the right which leads up into Glas Coire and soon you join the estate road coming up from Invermark. This is not the most interesting valley in Scotland, but a programme of planting

123

has been started with the intention of introducing some Scots pine and other native species to improve matters.

After 4km pass the Queen's Well. This is an odd feature, somewhat lacking in interest except that it was once visited by Queen Victoria. It is surrounded by an incongruous, rather ugly stone structure shaped like a crown. Full marks to Victoria for leaving her carriage and going for a walk, but one wonders what she made of this drab and rather barren place.

Shortly after passing the Queen's Well, you reach the last house in the valley – Glenmark. Here the climbing begins. The path winds up the heather-clad slopes of the Knowe of Crippley, for a time following the Ladder Burn. Gradually you rise above the burn, and the conical head of Mount Keen begins to peep above the head of the valley. Eventually the path – the Mounth Road, which is an ancient right of way – levels out on the broad plateau and cuts a sandy line through the heather on its way to Glen Tanar. As in many of the eastern Cairngorm hills the granite here is friable and has easily eroded to make stony, sandy, highly visible paths. At 40549 85247 (about 2½km beyond Glenmark House) a cairn marks the point where the path splits. Take the right fork, which goes directly to the top of **Mount Keen**. The summit is a jumble of granite blocks which give good views of the Lochnagar Hills to the west and the North Sea to the east (40904 86919) (3hrs).

Return by the same route.

ROUTE 29
Ben More (Isle of Mull) (966m)

Pronunciation: *Ben More*
Translation: *Big Mountain*

Distance:	12½km
Ascent:	1050m
Time:	4hrs 35mins
Difficulty:	scrambling (grade 1) on the east ridge; some exposure
Maps:	OS sheet 48; Explorer map 375; Area Map 3
Parking:	off-road at mouth of the Abhainn na h-Uamha
	GR: 50735 36829
Start:	faint path along southwest side of burn
Hostel:	YHA Tobermory; Independent Aros
B&B/hotel:	Salen; Tobermory
Camping:	Pennygown, about 3km east of Salen
Access:	Mckinnons, tel: 01631 563617

Ben More on Mull is a fine hill with an interesting ridge on its eastern side which gives an excellent easy scramble. The views along the way are extremely pleasant, and there is much interesting wildlife to be seen.

Park on an area of flat grass by the stone bridge at the outlet of the Abhainn na h-Uamha. Follow the burn pleasantly up through the Gleann na Beinne Fada. There is a faint path, rather wet at times, on the southwest side of the burn. After 2½km, where two burns join at 52866 34881, cross over to the northeast side and continue up a little rib, climbing towards the lowest point of the col. Climb south from the col over ground which is stony and

Mull has become a prime location for the white-tailed sea eagle, which now breeds here after a successful reintroduction of this species into Scotland in 1975. It is worth bringing a pair of binoculars and spending a little time on the coastal road round Loch na Keal so that you can look for these spectacular birds feeding in the loch. There are also seals and otters to be seen here. There are various ways to reach the island of Mull. The cheapest is by ferry from Lochaline to Fishnish – this route involves a fairly long drive but there are frequent sailings through the day and no booking is required. The ferry from Oban takes longer and needs to be booked in advance. The operator in both cases is Caledonian Macbrayne, tel: 01475 650100.

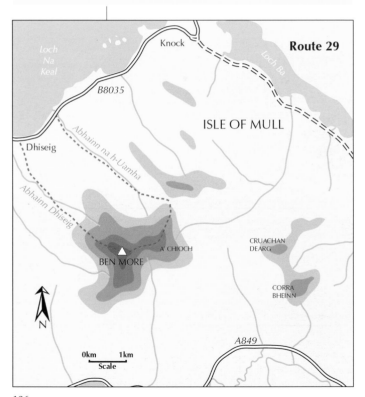

Corra Bheinn and the Southeast ridge of A' Chioch, Isle of Mull

increasingly rocky. There are little sections of easy scrambling, but no real difficulty, as the ridge steepens towards the top and the path dodges around more awkward rocks. Pass the summit cairn at 53499 33340 then continue westwards on an obvious path that drops down through rocks to reach the east ridge of **Ben More**. Quite a bit of height has to be lost before the ridge narrows dramatically and rises again. There is then some very pleasant walking and scrambling along the narrow ridge to the top.

The sharp, knife-edge arête can be bypassed by a path on the left of the crest that goes on to traverse the southern flanks of the ridge. This peters out on steep ground some way below the summit. If you stay on this path you'll need to retrace your steps for a short distance when the path peters out, then find the easiest line to scramble much more steeply directly up to the top. It is much better to stay on or close to the crest, which is an exhilarating but easy scramble, steepening towards the top. There is a stone enclosure at the summit at 52578 33070 (3hrs 25mins).

Descend easily via the northwest ridge, where there is a substantial cairned path for most of the way down. This is the 'standard' way up, and is the only side of the hill that most visitors see. Ben More is a popular hill for tourists and on a pleasant day you'll pass lots of them plodding dutifully up this scree-covered path from Dhiseig. Be warned, however, a compass bearing taken from the summit enclosure is likely to be inaccurate as the rocks here are highly magnetic. There are other parts of the mountain, too, where a compass bearing may be unreliable. If you need to take a bearing, take two or three from different points; this should help you to judge the effects of any magnetic variation. At 50785 34432 there is an easy crossing of the Abhainn Dhiseig, and a direct line back to the day's starting point can be made across the foot of An Gearna. This soon runs into deep, awkward grass, however, and it is doubtful whether much time is saved by cutting off this corner rather than continuing on the path to Dhiseig.

ROUTE 30
BEINN A' BHEITHIR

Sgorr Dhonuill (1001m),
Sgorr Dhearg (1024m)

Pronunciation: *Bine yer Veeyersh; Skor Ghorneel; Skor Jerrack*
Translation: *Hill of the Thunderbolt;*
Peak of the Donalds; Red Peak

Distance:	12km
Ascent:	1200m
Time:	5hrs 30mins
Difficulty:	some exposed scrambling (grade 1) on the northeast ridge
Maps:	OS sheet 41; Explorer map 384; Area Map 4
Parking:	car park in South Ballachulish at 04718 58949. (If doing the circuit in reverse, park close to the school in Ballachulish.)
Start:	from car park head south along gated forestry track
Hostel:	YHA Glencoe; Independent Glencoe
B&B/hotel:	Ballachulish or North Ballachulish
Camping:	Glen Coe
Access:	Forest Enterprise, tel: 01631 566155

This fine mountain really catches the eye in sunshine in the late afternoon as you cross the bridge at Ballachulish. Its deeply etched corries and strong ridges of Appin quartzite and Ballachulish limestone offer a first-class walk despite the heavy fringes of spruce around its northern flanks.

From the A828 turn off to South Ballachulish following the road to a small car park just before where the road is gated and it turns into a forestry track (04718 58949). The

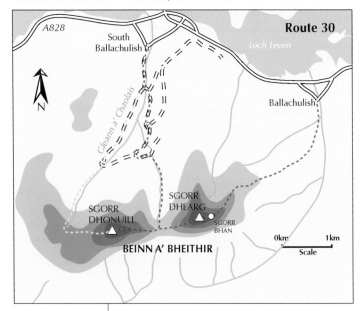

forest tracks here are not well represented on some current maps. About 200m past the Grannoch water treatment plant, turn left off the main track to cross the burn. The green track beyond climbs steadily uphill to join a bigger track higher up. Turn right onto this and about ¾km further on turn left to reach a concrete bridge over a burn. A more direct route that seems to reach this point from a turning a few hundred metres above the first bridge is in fact very overgrown, especially higher up.

The concrete bridge can also be reached by continuing on the main track past the water treatment plant, keeping the burn to your left (east). Continue on the main track round the head of the valley, almost doubling back along the contours for a while. Then take a right fork where the track branches to reach the concrete bridge.

Just beyond the concrete bridge is a cairn marking the start of the footpath at 04750 56934. This slippery steep path leads through the trees and eventually reaches a stile at 05038 56520. Cross the stile and continue on the path, which turns sharply to the right and follows the line of trees, then the line of an old fence. Some of the ground here can get very wet, and the worst of this can be avoided by a small detour to the left. Eventually arrive at the col (04803 55454) (2hrs).

Climb the narrowing ridge on a clear path to the summit cairn of **Sgorr Dhonuill** (04064 55530). The path keeps promising great exposure but never quite delivers on the promise, although it does have some fine positions (2hrs 45mins). An alternative ascent can be made by following the main forestry track past the water treatment plant right up to the head of the valley. From the bend a footpath leads up onto the ridge to the west of the summit and the ridge can be followed easily to the top from here.

Retrace your steps to the col and then head up the broad, stony west ridge of **Sgorr Dhearg**. The path is obvious, though it doesn't quite emulate Sgorr Dhonuill's fine ridge. The summit cairn is reached at 05687 55831 (3hrs 45mins).

*Beinn a' Bheithir –
Sgorr Dhonuill from
the north*

There is a range of options for the descent. The simplest and most boring of these is to return to the col and retrace your steps to South Ballachulish through the forest. The better alternatives continue on the curving ridge to the west-southwest to reach the summit cairn of Sgorr Bhan at 06275 56043. From this cairn descend 300m to a point where the path diverges. You can then head northwest, then north-northeast over Beinn Bhan and on down the north-northeast ridge, skirting the trees below, to arrive in Ballachulish.

But the best option by far if you like your walks to be exhilarating is to take the right fork where the path diverges and climb down the superb, sharp northeast ridge that leads directly back to the school at Ballachulish. Looking down this ridge in swirling mist the route appears fairly intimidating, but it is well worth the effort and not nearly as difficult as it appears. There are some short sections of scrambling in the upper part of the ridge, however, one 12ft section of which is quite steep, though on very good holds. For comparison it is both easier and less exposed than the scrambling on the Aonach Eagach. Stay on the crest of the ridge throughout. Do not be tempted to bypass the rocky sections on the steep, loose scree and dangerous ground that fall away on either side. Gradually the difficulties pass and the ridge eases gently over meadows to the path that emerges by the school. An exhilarating day out on an excellent ridge.

Those of a nervous disposition might prefer to tackle this route in reverse, starting from Ballachulish, so that their eyes can be fixed forever upwards on the ridge and they don't have to stare into the awful abyss…

ROUTE 31

AONACH EAGACH

Meall Dearg (953m),

Sgorr nam Fiannaidh (967m)

Pronunciation: *Ernoch Egg-yoch;*
Miaowl Jerrack; Skor num Feeonly
Translation: *Notched Ridge; Red Hill; Peak of the Fingalians*

Distance:	7km (plus return along the road)
Ascent:	1030m
Time:	5hrs (plus return along the road)
Difficulty:	exposed scrambling (grade 3) along the ridge; no escape from this route once the ridge is started. Great care needed in descent.
Maps:	OS sheet 41; Explorer map 384; Harvey's Superwalker map Glen Coe; Area Map 4
Parking:	lay-by on north side of A82
Start:	footpath from lay-by
Hostel:	YHA Glencoe; Independent Glencoe
B&B/hotel:	Glencoe; Balachulish
Camping:	Glen Coe
Access:	the main route is on land owned by the National Trust for Scotland. The land to the west of Sgorr nam Fiannaidh, below the Pap of Glencoe, is pivately owned farmland. NTS, tel: 01855 811729. There is an award-winning visitor centre – worth a visit – lower down the pass.

From the lay-by a few hundred metres below (and to the west of) the cottages of Allt na Reigh, follow the well-trodden path up towards Am Bodach. Although the steep corrie can be climbed to the east of Am Bodach, a better route is to follow the path that winds steeply up through

The great notched ridge – or Aonach Eagach – enclosing the northern side of the Pass of Glencoe, is one of the best-known and best-loved ridges in Britain. On a fine weekend in summer it is not unusual to find upwards of 20 or 30 parties enjoying its delights. Early arrival is advised if you hope to use one of the nearby parking places and avoid queuing on the pinnacles.

To the average hillwalker the Aonach Eagach poses a testing challenge. It is unlike other Munros outside of Skye, calling for a good head for heights on a number of exposed sections and the ability to move safely on rock. The scrambling is not nearly as difficult as many walkers fear, however, and very few parties will resort to using a rope, although inexperienced scramblers would be wise to join forces with someone who has experience. A rope should be carried by an experienced leader if there are any in the party who have doubts about their ability to scramble safely in exposed positions.

This route is serious and committing in that there are no safe lines of descent between Am Bodach and Sgorr nam Fiannaidh. The ridge is normally traversed from east to west, and at busy times it would be hard to justify doing it in reverse. Route-finding along the ridge is rarely a problem. Whilst there are often different options for circumventing problems, the main route is all too obvious from the line of scratches caused by the passage of innumerable crampons and axes.

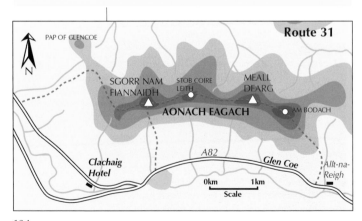

rocky terrain to Am Bodach's southeast ridge. This calls for some easy scrambling on the way to the summit at 16841 58025.

Descend west to reach a short, steep section which is taken on its right (north) side. There are plentiful handholds and a series of little ledges which aid progress. Pass back to the left and drop down again in a curving line to reach the crest of the ridge. An old iron fence post marks the way. Continue more easily along the narrow crest of the ridge to the first Munro, **Meall Dearg**, at 16136 58373 (2hrs 35mins).

Beyond Meall Dearg the ridge rises and falls over a series of small pinnacles which offer continuously interesting scrambling. Some short pitches are quite exposed. The nature of the scrambling is very diverse, with chimneys, slabs and a couple of small rock towers to overcome. Although care is required throughout this section, the rhyolite rock is mostly sound and reliable, with good holds appearing wherever they are needed. Nowhere are the difficulties very great, which means the route can be savoured and enjoyed. A steep pull onto Stob Coire Leith marks the end of the scrambling, and from here there is easy walking to the second Munro, **Sgorr nam Fiannaidh**, at 14049 58302 (4hrs 10mins).

All problems are not yet behind you, however, as great care needs to be taken on the descent. The most

*Aonach Eagach
in winter*

direct descent from the summit of Sgorr nam Fiannaidh is due south down an eroded path which is continuously steep and, at the top, very loose. Dislodged stones can pose a serious risk to people below. Another path leads down the west side of the Clachaig gully. This again is steep and loose, with the added problem of some slabby rock to descend and considerable exposure at times. This route is no longer recommended as the loose rock here poses a real danger to people below, especially to climbers in the gully who may not be visible to parties in descent. The safest and easiest descent takes a slightly longer line, continuing along the main ridge to the col below the Pap of Glencoe. From here a path leads south-west to reach the minor road to Glencoe village.

Return along the road.

ROUTE 32

Bidean nam Bian (1150m),

Stob Coire Sgreamhach (1072m)

Pronunciation: *Beed-yan nam Ee-yann;*
Stob Korrer Skrevuch
Translation: *Chief of the Hills; Peak of the Fearful Corrie*

Bidean is a beautiful but dark, secretive mountain whose summit is jealously guarded behind the Three Sisters of Glen Coe and Stob Coire nan Lochan (which in any other company would be a Munro in its own right). It may be climbed from various directions, but the most popular approach is from the A82 between Achtriochtan and Allt-na-reigh.

From the car park drop down to the wooden bridge that crosses the River Coe and then climb sharply up into the steep-sided Coire nan Lochan. To your right is a climber's playground – the east face of Aonach Dubh; the rhyolite lava flows that make up these cliffs give some excellent steep climbs. Continue steadily upwards to the head of

Distance:	11km
Ascent:	1030m
Time:	5hrs
Difficulty:	one or two sections of simple scrambling (up to grade 1), much of which is avoidable
Maps:	OS sheet 41; Explorer map 384; Harvey's Superwalker map Glen Coe; Area Map 4
Parking:	main car park below Allt-na-reigh on A82
Start:	footpath crosses River Coe from car park
Hostel:	YHA Glen Coe; Independent Glencoe
B&B/hotel:	Glencoe/Ballachulish
Camping:	Glen Coe
Access:	National Trust for Scotland, tel: 01855 811729. There is a visitor centre – worth a visit – accessed from the A82.

To the south of Glen Coe is an area of towering rocky mountains with dramatic ridges and fine hanging valleys. One of these valleys – the Lost Valley – was reputedly a hiding place for cattle stolen by the Macdonalds. Further down the valley, Meall Mor was the hill they fled to in the dark of night during the winter snows of 1692 when the massacre began at the hands of the Campbells and their homes were put to the torch. Somehow the history sets the tone for these huge, brooding hills.

the corrie where steep walls seem to prevent any escape. The path continues straight up the headwall, staying to the left of the burn and the small waterfall in its upper reaches.

You eventually emerge into a wide upper corrie enclosed by two of the outstretched ridges of Stob Coire nan Lochan. Either ridge can be climbed and both of them make pleasant ascents amid spectacular mountain scenery. To climb the east ridge turn left and head south-east up a short slope to gain the crest of the ridge at 15502 55017, then follow this either on its crest or on the

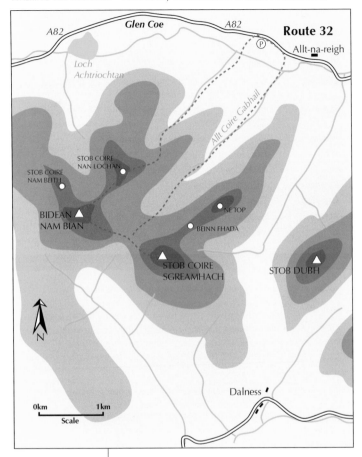

path which stays mostly on its left (south) side. Higher up it becomes rocky and bouldery with some easy scrambling before reaching the summit cairn at 14837 54857 (2hrs 35mins).

Descend over boulders to the southwest col of Bidean (which offers an escape – steep at first – down to the Lost Valley). Then continue up the ridge to the summit

of **Bidean nam Bian**. The path winds between rocks and avoids some of the jumbled blocks near the top of the ridge, although these can be climbed quite pleasantly to the top. Once the angle eases there is a short walk to the summit cairn at 14347 54200 (2hrs 50mins).

Aonach Dubh from Coire nan Lochan

From the top, head southeast for 1km along a ridge which becomes broad and easy, crossing a subsidiary minor top en route. Reach the col and from here climb easily to reach the summit of **Sgreamhach** at 15493 53654 (3hrs 40mins).

One route back from here crosses Beinn Fhada, then drops steeply back to Glencoe. Most parties, however, will chose to return by way of the Lost Valley. Retrace your steps to the col and descend steeply at first down a red, muddy, heavily eroded path that is quite enclosed for the first 15ft, like a little chute. It is essential to locate the correct point for descent as all the other gullies from this ridge are dangerous. A small cairn marks the point where the path begins at 15092 53677. Follow it down until the angle eases over a boulder field. Below this the path becomes clear again following the left side of the burn. At the huge boulders at the end of the Lost Valley, the path climbs slightly onto the right-hand side of the valley

The lost valley from Stob Coire Sgreamhach

before falling again. Shortly after dropping over a rocky section, the path splits. The left-hand branch crosses the stream at a point where it passes beneath some large boulders; the other branch crosses it lower down at a ford. If using this latter route at times of spate, it might be necessary to unboot or get wet. The two paths join up again before entering an area of woodland regeneration and crossing a bridge. From here a short walk leads back to the road.

ROUTE 33

BUACHAILLE ETIVE MOR

Stob Dearg (1022m),

Stob na Broige (956m)

Pronunciation: Booerchullah
Aytchyer Moar; Stob Jerrack; Stob na Brogg-yer
Translation: Big Herdsman of Etive; Red Peak; Lively Hill

Distance:	13km
Ascent:	1060m
Time:	5hrs
Difficulty:	some simple scrambling (grade 0.5) at the top of Coire na T Tulaich
Maps:	OS sheet 41; Explorer map 384; Harvey's Superwalker map Glen Coe; Area Map 4
Parking:	parking spaces off road
Start:	footpath from Altnafeadh on A82
Hostel:	YHA Glencoe; Independent Glencoe
B&B/hotel:	Kingshouse Hotel on Rannoch Moor; Glencoe
Camping:	Kingshouse Hotel on Rannoch Moor; Glen Coe
Access:	National Trust for Scotland, tel:01855 811729

'The Buachaille', as it is affectionately called, is one of the best-known and most photographed mountains in Scotland. It is a Mecca for climbers as well as walkers, with some fine steep routes on Rannoch Wall and excellent friction climbing on the granite of the Etive Slabs. There are not many easy ways onto the ridge, or off it, but this adds to the atmosphere of the place, and the views in all directions on a clear day will not easily be forgotten.

Cars may be left off the road at Altnafeadh, and from here a short walk takes you over the River Coupall and past the little white cottage of Lagangarbh. About 100m past the cottage the footpath splits. Take the right fork and follow it, rising slowly, all the way to Coire na Tulaich, which offers an obvious break in the impressive rock buttresses on this side of the hill. The scree-filled gully may be climbed fairly directly, with one small section of easy scrambling higher up. Alternatively there is a path that tries to find easier ground above the gully bed, mostly on the right. The gully narrows and steepens higher up and at the very top it is necessary to leave it altogether, taking to the easy rocks on its left-hand side to

141

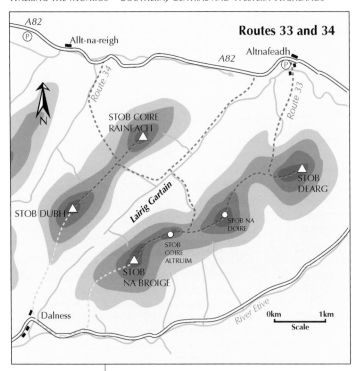

emerge after a little easy scrambling at a wide col on the main ridge, just below the final slopes of Stob Dearg. In winter the top of the gully may be corniced, and indeed the gully itself is prone to avalanche. There have been a number of winter fatalities here. Turn to the east and climb over shattered rocks for about ¾km to the summit of **Stob Dearg** (22365 54311) (2hrs).

There are fine views from the summit of Stob Dearg across Rannoch Moor, taking in the Nevis range, the Aonachs, the Grey Corries, Easain and Mheadhoin and many other hills. Retrace your steps to the col then follow the ridge past the small top at 903m and veer to the southwest until a sharp rise takes you to the top of Stob

na Doire 20758 53258. At 1011m this peak is only a little smaller than Stob Dearg and it also gives fine views. From here the path drops sharply down a rocky arête to a col below Stob Coire Altruim. Stay on the crest of the ridge. From the col climb Stob Coire Altruim to the cairn at 19805 53072 and continue pleasantly along the ridge to the next Munro: **Stob na Broige** at 19074 52554 (3hrs 30mins).

The best line of descent is from the col between Stob Coire Altruim and Stob na Doire. Retrace your steps to this col and drop quite sharply at first towards the Lairig Gartain. The start of the descent path is marked by a small cairn at 20060 52902. The path drops towards the River Coupall, then follows this back to Altnafeadh.

Strong parties, however, may wish to combine this route with the next one by continuing to the far southwestern end of the ridge and descending from there to Glen Etive. Return can then be made to Altnafeadh by

The ridge of Buachaille Etive Mor with Stob Dubh behind and Bidean nam Bian on skyline

way of Buachaille Etive Beag, reversing Route 34. This makes for a long but rewarding day with over 2000m of vertical ascent (20km, 8hrs 15mins). To do this, continue from Stob na Broige in a southwesterly direction, dropping down over easy grassy slopes to a small outlying hill at the end of the ridge. This hill is not immediately visible when you start the descent. Just before you reach it, at a grassy col, turn southeast (18010 51960). A broad, grass-filled gully drops quite steeply down from here. The descent from here is not particularly pleasant.

Perhaps the best line down from the col is to stay towards the right-hand side of the grass gully, and after a short while to cross the burn at its right-hand edge. Then cross over a projecting spur and descend the last ½km towards the southwest. The final slope is covered in deep grass which conceals pot-holes and rocks. Eventually bracken and more grass lead to the road. Once on the road turn right to 17102 51501, where a gate leads directly onto the southwest flanks of Stob Dubh. Ignore the path that leads over the Lairig Gartain and ascend the

Summit of Stob Dearg

nose of Stob Dubh direct. It is a fairly relentless climb to the summit, the last 250m of which is over scree and broken rocks.

Ben Nevis and surrounding hills from Stob Dearg

ROUTE 34

BUACHAILLE ETIVE BEAG
Stob Dubh (958m),
Stob Coire Raineach (925m)

Pronunciation: *Booerchullah Aytcher Bayk; Stob Doo; Stob Korrer Ran-yoch*
Translation: *Little Herdsman of Etive; Dark Peak; Peak of the Corrie of Ferns*

This is the smaller brother of Buachaille Etive Mor and, whilst still offering a shapely ridge with spectacular views, it is lower in altitude and offers an easier outing than its more celebrated neighbour.

There are three possible lines of approach: from the southwest, by the route described above; from the

145

Distance:	9km
Ascent:	880m
Time:	5hrs 10mins
Maps:	OS sheet 41; Explorer map 384; Harvey's Superwalker map Glen Coe; Area Map 4; see Route 33 for sketch map
Parking:	lay-by on the A82 just east of the Study, or car park at Altnafeadh
Start:	footpath to col
Hostel:	YHA Glencoe; Independent Glen Coe
B&B/hotel:	Kingshouse Hotel on Rannoch Moor; Glen Coe
Camping:	Kingshouse Hotel; Glen Coe
Access:	National Trust for Scotland, tel: 01855 811729

northwest; and from the southeast. These latter two routes start on the A82 and both arrive at the same point on the col below Stob Coire Raineach. From the car park just to the east of the Study on the A82 (where the road cuts through rocks) follow a path signposted 'Lairig Eilde to Glen Etive'. This path soon crosses the burn – the Allt Lairig Eilde. Before it does, however, another path leads off to the left (south) and leads up the hillside around Stob Coire Raineach to the col.

If starting from the car park at Altnafeadh, follow the A82 west for just under 1km to pick up a muddy path that leads alongside the River Coupall. At 19505 53952 a faint path leads up alongside a small burn directly up the grassy slope to the col. This path disappears higher up.

From the col it is a short climb up the ridge to the good summit views of **Stob Coire Raineach** at 19138 54790 (2hrs 35mins).

Return to the col, avoiding several small scree slopes that drop away steeply to the west. From the col it is a straightforward climb along the ridge over an unnamed minor top to **Stob Dubh** at the far end of the ridge. The summit cairn is at 17914 53534 (3hrs 35mins).

Return by any of the routes described.

ROUTE 35
Beinn Sgulaird (937m)

Pronunciation: Bine Skoolarge
Translation: Mountain of the Old Hat

Distance:	12km
Ascent:	1100m
Time:	4hrs 50mins
Maps:	OS sheet 50; Explorer maps 384 and 377; Area Map 4
Parking:	lay-by just north of Druimavuic, Glen Creran
Start:	private track leads through trees from the road to the hillside
Hostel:	YHA Oban; Independent Oban
B&B/hotel:	Port Appin; Connel; Oban
Camping:	Barcaldine by Loch Creran
Access:	Glencreran, tel: 01631 730312

Beinn Sgulaird is an interesting but fairly solitary hill to the east of Glen Creran. The circular walk described here makes a fine day's outing.

A combination of deer fencing and private roads means there are really only two points of access to this hill. The first involves parking at Elleric at the end of the public road and crossing the River Ure at Glenure to make a steep, direct ascent from the west. The other, more pleasant and varied and also more popular, starts from Drumavuic, as described here.

Park in the lay-by on the minor road just north of Druimavuic. As you walk towards Druimavuic two tracks

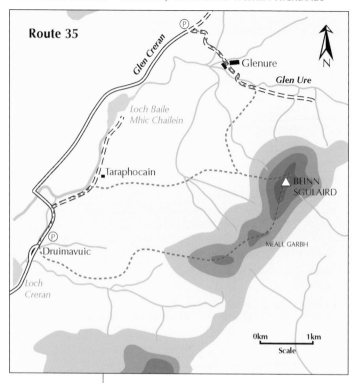

lead off this road to the left. The first leads through trees and out onto the open hill. The second leads up to the house. Follow the first track through a gate and uphill at the extreme southwest end of Sgulaird's long ridge. When the track reaches a highpoint on the ridge, before it curves out of sight into the valley of the Allt Buidhe, a small cairn marks the start of a faint path that leads up the crest of the ridge. Follow this to the far side of the first hill – Point 488 – where there is a 40m drop. Then climb again over springy grass until the ground becomes more bouldery near the top of the next hill at 863m. There is a cairn here at 04287 44795. Next drop down to the

Starting the descent from Beinn Sgulaird

northeast to a col; the descent is down a steep, boulder-strewn slope, losing about 70m in height. Then climb again to another top at 848m. From here there is yet another sharp drop, first down a scree-filled gully to the left, then back to the right down a steep, bouldery slope to reach a narrow col. From this col it is a straightforward climb to **Beinn Sgulaird**'s substantial summit cairn at 05306 46081 (2hrs 50mins).

To descend, either retrace the route of ascent, or continue to the northeast to the head of a rocky valley. This can be descended first to the northwest, then by veering southwest down a steep grassy slope to reach an old stone shieling and sheep pen – clearly visible from above, though not marked on the OS map – at 03256 46491. From here a grassy track leads back through the trees just south of Taraphocain to emerge on the private road by some animal pens.

ROUTE 36

Sgor na h-Ulaidh (994m)

Pronunciation: *Skor na Hoolee*
Translation: *Peak of the Treasure*

Distance:	14km
Ascent:	940m
Time:	5hrs
Maps:	OS sheets 41 and 50; Explorer map 384; Harvey's Superwalker map Glen Coe; Area Map 4
Parking:	room for a few vehicles by the bridge just north of Invercharnan
Start:	along private track past house at Invercharnan
Hostel:	YHA Glencoe; Independent Glencoe
B&B/hotel:	Kingshouse Hotel; Glencoe
Camping:	Kingshouse Hotel; Glencoe
Access:	tel: 01855 851277

Bidean nam Bian from Sgor na h-Ulaidh

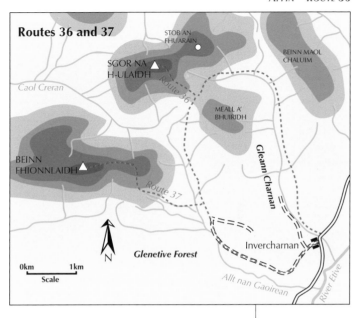

Routes 36 and 37

STOB AN
FHUARAIN

BEINN MAOL
CHALUIM

SGOR NA
H-ULAIDH

Caol Creran

Route 36

MEALL A'
BHUIRIDH

BEINN
FHIONNLAIDH

Route 37

Gleann Charnan

Invercharnan

0km   1km
Scale

N

Glenetive Forest

Allt nan Gaoirean

River Etive

As you drive down Glen Etive beyond Dalness, the big peaks to the east of the glen take centre stage whilst the high ground to its west is largely lost to view. The two hidden Munros in this stretch that are accessible from this road are Sgor na h-Ulaidh and Beinn Fhionnlaidh. Tucked away behind the great bulk of Bidean nam Bian and the other Glen Coe giants, Sgor na h-Ulaidh offers an interesting walk, quite steep at times, with some good views of its more celebrated neighbours.

Pass through the gate of Invercharnan and walk past the house and along the forest track for 3km, gradually gaining height. At 12129 48812, where the track makes an abrupt turn, branch off onto an obvious path that soon leads out of the trees and onto open hillside. Head across rough grass, staying well above the burn, and make for the col between Meall a' Bhuiridh and Sgor na h-Ulaidh.

151

Sgor na h-Ulaidh from Beinn Fhionnlaidh

The path quickly disappears once the trees are left behind. The col itself is not always visible, but if you head for the lowest visible point between the two hills you won't go far wrong. The southeast ridge of Sgor na h-Ulaidh is steep and quite rocky. There are two or three possible lines of ascent through the rocks, but the easiest is probably from the back of the wide col, where a faint and intermittent path can be found leading through the rocks, quite steeply at times, to the top. Right at the top, join the prominent path that comes up from Glencoe over Stob an Fhuarain and admire some excellent views of Bidean and other surrounding hills. The **Sgor na h-Ulaidh** summit cairn is at 11120 51786 (3hrs 15mins).

Return by the same route unless you wish to include Beinn Fhionnlaidh (see Route 37) in the day's outing. It is also possible to make an alternative descent to the northeast from the col at 11810 51315 into the glacier-sculpted valley of the Allt Charnan. Wind around this curved valley for about 3km, crossing a number of small burns to reach a path through the trees that returns directly to the bridge at the day's starting point.

ROUTE 37

Beinn Fhionnlaidh (959m)

Pronunciation: *Bine Ee-yoon-lie*
Translation: *Finlay's Mountain*

Distance:	13km
Ascent:	960m
Time:	4hrs 40mins
Maps:	OS sheet 50; Explorer map 384; Area Map 4; see Route 36 for sketch map
Parking:	by the bridge just north of Invercharnan
Start:	along private track past Invercharnan
Hostel:	YHA Glencoe; Independent Glencoe
B&B/hotel:	Kingshouse Hotel; Glencoe
Camping:	Kingshouse Hotel
Access:	tel: 01855 851277

Beinn Fhionnlaidh is occasionally climbed from Glenure in Glen Creran via its long west ridge, but it can equally well be approached from Glen Etive, as described here. This secretive hill is often overlooked by hillwalkers in this area, but it gives a pleasant and worthwhile outing.

Beinn Sgulaird from Beinn Fionnlaidh

Start as for the previous route, passing between the buildings of Invercharnan and following the forest track to the open hillside. Unfortunately the dreaded rhododendron weed has been allowed to colonize the whole length of this track. This shrub is not native to Britain, it spreads rapidly, is almost impossible to eradicate and is damaging to local wildlife. Turn left at the fence by the edge of the trees and drop down a short distance to cross a burn – the Allt nan Gaoirean – on a rickety bridge. You may feel safer crossing on boulders in the bed of the burn.

Continue uphill alongside another burn that flows down an obvious gash in the hillside just north of Meall nan Gobhar. Cross to the north side of this burn and climb alongside it to the top of the gash. From here climb steeply up the ridge of Beinn Fhionnlaidh's eastern outpost – marked only as Point 841 on the OS map. The highest point of this top doesn't have to be reached. Instead you can veer off before the top to the left (west) to reach a small col between the two tops, then climb **Beinn Fhionnlaidh**'s rocky east ridge to its summit. There are a couple of easy scrambling moves to contend with (avoidable on the left) before the summit cairn and trig point are reached at 09503 49764 (3hrs).

Return by the same route.

Beinn Fionnlaidh summit looking west

ETIVE

ROUTE 38

Ben Starav (1078m),
Beinn nan Aighenan (957m),
Glas Bheinn Mhor (997m)

Pronunciation: Ben Starav; Bine Ner-nigh-yan; Glaz Vine Voar
Translation: Mountain of the Rustling Noise, or of the Block
of Rock; Mountain of the Hinds; Big Grey-green Mountain

Distance:	20km
Ascent:	1820m
Time:	7hrs 50mins
Maps:	OS sheet 50; Explorer maps 377 and 384; Harvey's Superwalker map Glen Coe; Area Map 4
Parking:	roadside 3km from the southwest end of Glen Etive
Start:	along private track across river
Hostel:	YHA Glencoe; Independent Glencoe
B&B/hotel:	Kingshouse Hotel on A82 at head of valley
Camping:	Glen Coe
Access:	Blackmount Estate, tel: 01855 851277 and West Highland Estate, tel: 01866 822271. Blackmount Estate request that during the stag stalking season walkers keep to the route described here. This means avoiding the paths that follow the Allt nam Meirteach and the corrie immediately to its east. This would mean that at this time of year Beinn nan Aighenan could not be climbed on its own from this direction.

Follow the track across the River Etive and pass the old cottage at Colleitir, then continue on the south side of the River Etive along a path that leads to a bridge over the Allt Mheuran. Cross this and follow the path for a short distance until the nose of Ben Starav's long north ridge is

155

This group of hills sit together in some splendid countryside at the south-western end of Glen Etive. Together they make a memorable walk over interesting and varied terrain, and the outing described here is rightly regarded as one of the classic outings in this part of Scotland. There is no practicable approach to these hills from any other direction without a very long walk-in, perhaps combined with some wild camping nearby.

Tackling all three of these hills in one outing gives a fairly long but satisfying day with quite a lot of vertical metres to climb. An alternative would be to save Beinn nan Aighenan for a separate outing (but see note above about access). A much longer variation could be made by linking this route to Route 39, but only the fittest and most determined of parties should consider taking on such a challenge.

Beinn nan Aighenan from Ben Starav

reached. At this point leave the main path and begin the fairly arduous 3km climb up the crest of the ridge. There is a clear path all the way up, the last couple of hundred metres being over boulder scree. **Ben Starav**'s summit cairn is at 12578 42705. From the top there are good views across Loch Etive and beyond (3hrs).

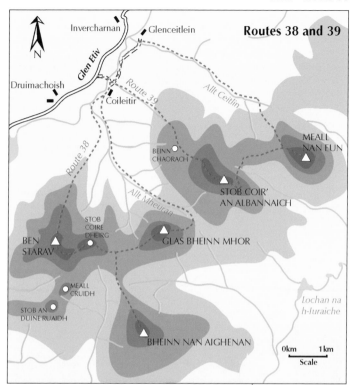

Routes 38 and 39

Follow the rim of Ben Starav's rocky northeastern corrie, passing a small cairned point then dropping steeply down the far side of the horseshoe. The ridge narrows over the next section and becomes quite a sharp rocky arête; however there is no technical difficulty. Reach the cairn on Stob Coire Dheirg (more good views) and from here head east down the rest of the ridge to a col at 766m. From the col descend on a southeasterly traverse around the west flank of Meall nan Tri Tighearnan to reach a rough, boulder-strewn col beneath the rugged north ridge of **Beinn nan Aighenan**. Climb this ridge, which is quite steep and rocky in places, to the summit.

157

Ghlas Bheinn Mhor from Stob Coire Dhoire

In winter, in poor visibility, this remote summit could be an awkward place to reach and the return journey could be equally tricky. In summer, however, a path makes route-finding straightforward. The summit cairn is at 14851 40519 (4hrs 35mins).

Once you have topped out on Beinn nan Aighenan there is no option but to return all the way to the 766m col. From here climb easily up the little minor top of Meall nan Tri Tighearnan, passing its cairn at 14543 42550, then drop down a short distance before the final climb of the day up the ridge to **Glas Bheinn Mhor** at 15335 42972 (6hrs 20mins).

To descend, drop gently off the summit to the east and cross a flat section of the ridge, then drop steeply down a rocky path to a narrow col which is just over 1km from the summit of Glas Bheinn Mhor. From here a stalker's path leads down alongside the Allt Mheuran and this is followed on the northeast side of the burn all the way back to Colleitir and the bridge over the River Etive.

ROUTE 39

Stob Coir' an Albannaich (1044m),

Meall nan Eun (928m)

Pronunciation: *Stob Korrer Nalabaneech; Miaowl nun Yeean*
Translation: *Peak of the Corrie*
of the Scotsman; Hill of the Birds

These two tough hills can be tackled as part of a greater traverse of the Ben Starav/Glas Bheinn Mhor excursion described above (Route 38). However, it will take a fit and determined party to complete such a long and gruelling route in one day. The two hills, which are rather disparate in nature, can also be approached by a very long walk-in from Victoria Bridge. However, they are more usually climbed as a separate outing from Glen Etive, starting from the same point as the Ben Starav circuit.

Distance:	15km
Ascent:	1240m
Time:	5hrs 50mins
Maps:	OS sheet 50; Explorer maps 377 and 384; Harvey's Superwalker map Glen Coe; Area Map 4; see Route 38 for sketch map
Parking:	roadside, close to the track that crosses River Etive to Coileitir
Start:	follow private track over river
Hostel:	YHA Glencoe; Independent Glencoe
B&B/hotel:	Kingshouse Hotel; Glencoe
Camping:	Kingshouse Hotel
Access:	Strutt and Parker, tel: 01330 824888 or Dalness Estate, tel: 01855 851274

Cross the bridge and take the first turning on the left after just a few metres. A few metres further on a gate leads into a pretty plantation of birch trees. A faint path leads up through the plantation on the left (north) side of the burn that flows almost from the very top of Beinn Chaorach. Follow this, crossing a gate at the upper edge of the plantation, and continue on the left side of this burn all the way to the top. Seen from the road below, the burn cuts an obvious, deep, tree-filled gash straight down the hillside. It is a steep and fairly relentless climb, but not nearly as bad as it looks head-on from below. (It is perhaps worth seeking out the interesting granite pavement scattered with small erratic stones – a 'De'ils Bowling Green' left over from the last Ice Age – almost due south from Beinn Chaorach's cairned summit.) At the top, veer round to the south to bypass crags formed by the burn that flows down into Coire Glas, then climb more gently for another 1½km to the summit cairn of **Stob Coir' an Albannaich** (16959 44289) (3hrs).

After admiring the views from the top of Stob Coir' an Albannaich, continue down its southeast ridge, which narrows and drops quite steeply for a short distance. A lot

of deep snow tends to gather on this ridge and this can sometimes linger long into spring. After ½km the ridge begins to level out and a small cairn marks the start of a grassy route leading down through the steep, slabby rocks of the north face to reach a broad, rough col beneath Meall Tarsuinn. It is important not to leave the ridge too soon when descending to this col as there is much dangerous ground on Stob Coir' an Albannaich's steep north face. Climb easily over Meall Tarsuinn, and after a short drop continue gently upwards to the summit of **Meall nan Eun** – a fairly unimpressive Munro which crouches tamely between much bigger hills on either side. The summit cairn lies well over to the east of the plateau at 19232 44907 (4hrs 10mins).

To descend, return across the plateau and drop quite steeply down the northwest flanks of the hill into the Coirean Riabhach, avoiding any awkward rocks, to reach a path along the north bank of the Allt Ceitlein. This returns you to the track over the River Etive and the day's starting point.

Stob Coir' an Albannaich

BLACKMOUNT

ROUTE 40

Creise (1100m),

Meall a' Bhuiridh (1108m)

Pronunciation: *Kereesha; Miaowl uh Vooree*
Translation: *Origin unclear; Hill of the Roaring (Stags)*

When driving along the A82 towards the Pass of Glencoe, the eye dances over the watery magic of Rannoch Moor and is then transfixed by the startling profile of Buachaille Etive Mor. The horseshoe of hills to the east of the Buachaille, on the opposite side of Glen Etive, are easy to overlook in such company and are better known for their ski tows than their walking. When seen from Kingshouse, however, in the evening sunlight, Sron na Creise can make an imposing spectacle.

The quickest and easiest way onto these hills is from the White Corries car park, climbing initially alongside the ski tows. However, in addition to being aesthetically marred by the ski paraphernalia, this route also involves retracing your steps on the return journey. A more interesting day can be had by starting up the steep north ridge of Sron na Creise and going round the horseshoe, returning via Creag Dhubh, although this requires a crossing of the River Etive and also involves some steep scrambling on the initial ascent.

The Blackmount and Glen Etive Ranger Service mark a route on their map from Blackrock Cottage around the nose of Creag Dhubh to reach the north ridge of Sron na Creise, but there are no paths along this boggy stretch of moor, and if you're intending to do the ridge and then the horseshoe, it is far better to start from Glen Etive.

There are two good places to cross the River Etive: one is just above its confluence with the River Coupall;

Distance:	10km
Ascent:	1320m
Time:	4hrs 45mins
Difficulty:	easy scrambling (grade 1 or less) on the connecting ridge between the two hills and on Sron na Creise if the easiest line is taken; up to grade 3 exposed scrambling possible if you are looking for difficulties on Sron na Creise
Maps:	OS sheet 41; Explorer map 384; Harvey's Superwalker map Glen Coe; Area Map 4
Parking:	lay-by in Glen Etive or White Corries car park
Start:	Cross the River Etive if you are including Sron na Creise or, if starting from the White Corries car park, start up through the ski tows
Hostel:	YHA Glencoe; Independent Glencoe
B&B/hotel:	Kingshouse Hotel on Rannoch Moor; Glen Coe
Camping:	Kingshouse Hotel on Rannoch Moor; Glen Coe
Access:	Blackmount Estates, tel: 01838 400255

the other is about 1km further downstream, almost directly opposite the start of the north ridge, where a profusion of large boulders in the river bed make natural stepping-stones. At times of heavy spate, however, all these boulders can be completely submerged and neither option may be possible.

The lower part of the ridge is punctuated by several small, greasy outcrops that can easily be bypassed. The higher rocks of the ridge can be avoided on the right for a while, but eventually your hands may be called into use (this is no more than grade 1 scrambling if the easiest line is taken). A steep and airy intermediate grade scramble is also possible if you prefer. There are numerous possibilities. From the top, cross Stob a' Ghlais Choire and follow the rocky ridge to reach the summit of **Creise** (not named on earlier OS maps) at 23861 50634 (2hrs 30mins).

Continue south for ½km to a small cairn on the edge of the corrie at 23892 50015. This marks the point of descent to the connecting ridge between Creise and

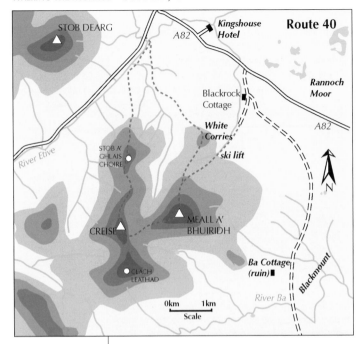

Meall a' Bhuiridh (left) and Creise (centre) from Stob Dearg

Creise from Kingshouse Hotel

Meall a' Bhuiridh. The correct line drops very steeply at first (but without difficulty) down the rocky arête, eventually crossing a col and then climbing quite steeply again up the rocky ridge to **Meall a' Bhuiridh** (25063 50340). There are fine views over Rannoch Moor from here. The stony summit of Meall a' Bhuiridh is sadly only a stone's throw from the top ski tow (3hrs 20mins).

Continue north along the bouldery slope, crossing a saddle and briefly climbing again to reach Point 749 on the map, before finally dropping down the northwest ridge of Creag Dhubh.

Those opting for the ascent from White Corries will find a path starting between the two buildings at the bottom of the ski tow. Climb to the top of this tow, then head southwest to the start of the next one, and finally go west to gain the broad ridge which leads to Meall a' Bhuiridh.

165

ROUTE 41

Stob a' Choire Odhair (945m),
Stob Ghabhar (1090m)

Pronunciation: *Stob a Horrer Ower; Stob Roo-er*
Translation: *Peak of the Grey-Brown Corrie; Goat Peak*

Distance:	16km
Ascent:	1170m
Time:	5hrs 30mins
Maps:	OS sheet 50; Explorer map 384; Harvey's Superwalker map Glen Coe; Area Map 4
Parking:	car park 1km beyond Inveroran Hotel, just before Victoria Bridge
Start:	cross the Victoria Bridge then turn left onto Estate track
Hostel:	YHA Crianlarich; Independent Tyndrum and Bridge of Orchy
B&B/hotel:	Inveroran Hotel; Bridge of Orchy; Tyndrum
Camping:	there may be some local camping – ask at Inveroran Hotel – otherwise Tyndrum or Kingshouse Hotel
Access:	Blackmount, tel: 01838 400255

These two old favourites sit close together on the southwestern edge of Rannoch Moor and, despite a fairly big loss of height between the two, are usually climbed together. The route described gives quite a tough but interesting hill walk with some superb views of Rannoch Moor.

From the car park head north across Victoria Bridge and turn left just before Forest Lodge on a track that goes alongside the Abhainn Shira. After 1½km leave the track at a green metal hut on a path that climbs alongside the Allt Toaig between Stob Ghabhar and Stob a' Choire Odhair. About 2km along this path, just after crossing a tributary burn, take to the hillside, climbing steeply up an obvious ridge to the left of a large gully. There is a path

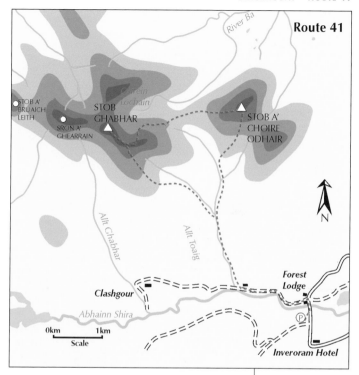

Route 41

that zigzags higher up before losing its way in stones and boulders near the top. Continue climbing straight up to the **Stob a' Choire Odhair** summit cairn at 25734 45974. Pause here to admire a grandstand view of Rannoch Moor (2hrs 40mins).

The way on to Stob Ghabhar is not immediately obvious from here. The link to the long curving ridge of Sron na Giubhas, which looks like a possible line of ascent, is barred by crags, a big loss of height and a river. In fact the easiest way on to Stob Ghabhar follows the line of the old county boundary, prominently marked on the OS map. Leave the summit of Stob a' Choire Odhair to the southwest, then veer round to the west to reach a

Rannoch Moor and Stob a' Choire Odhair from Stob Ghabhar

rough, rocky col after 1½km, then continue uphill on a line that swings round sharply to the south, climbing the steep flanks of the Aonach Eagach through boulders and scree to reach the top. From here continue more easily along the ridge, which becomes quite narrow for a while before rising to **Stob Ghabhar**'s rocky summit at 23024 45509 (4hrs).

To descend, take the most direct route back which retraces your steps to a small cairn marking the top of Stob Ghabhar's southeast ridge. Some old metal fence posts lead the way down this broad ridge. Lower down the path passes alongside the long ribbon of waterfalls that drop gracefully over Creag an Steallaire. This makes for a pleasant descent back to the outward path, which is joined after crossing the Allt Toaig.

Rannoch Moor from Stob a' Choire Odhair

169

BRIDGE OF ORCHY

ROUTE 42

Beinn Achaladair (1038m),

Beinn a' Chreachain (1081m)

Pronunciation: *Bine Achullader; Bine yuh Chrechen*
Translation: *Mountain of the*
Farm by the Water; Mountain of the Bare Summit

Distance:	18km
Ascent:	1230m
Time:	6hrs
Maps:	OS sheet 50; Explorer map 377; Area Map 4
Parking:	car park at Achallader Farm
Start:	through farm to footpath
Hostel:	YHA Crianlarich; Independent Tyndrum and Bridge of Orchy station
B&B/hotel:	Tyndrum
Camping:	Tyndrum
Access:	Blackmount Estate, tel: 01838 400255

These two fine hills rise up steeply above their bastion of north-facing cliffs on the southern edge of Rannoch Moor. They give wonderful views across the vast watery wasteland of the moor and there are fine views also to the hills of the Blackmount further west.

The easiest access to these hills is from Achallader Farm via a private road from the A82 at the east end of Loch Tulla. The landowners have kindly provided a car park adjacent to the farm itself for the use of walkers. From the car park, pass through the farm and head uphill on a

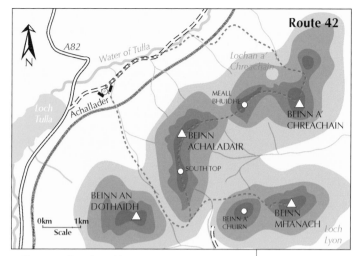

well-worn path to the col between Beinn Achaladair and Beinn an Dothaidh. This path crosses and recrosses the Allt Coire Achaladair without difficulty, and higher up passes an interesting section of waterfalls over striated rocks. Once the col is reached turn left (north) and climb

Beinn Achaladair summit ridge

grassy slopes on the crest of the ridge to the cairned southern top at 34230 42046. The walking is easy. Continue after a short drop to rise again to **Beinn Achaladair**'s main summit ridge. There are two cairned points, the first of which, although having a smaller cairn, is actually the highest point at 34350 43118 (3hrs).

From this airy viewpoint on a clear day you can take in a fine panorama. Looking east there are dramatic views towards your next objective – Beinn a' Chreachain – along the line of northwest-facing cliffs. Drop sharply but easily down a very steep section from Achaladair and begin the gradual rise over grassy slopes to Beinn a' Chreachain, passing first over a grassy minor top, Meall Buidhe. The path stays close to the top of the cliffs until the last steep climb to **Beinn a' Chreachain**'s stony summit at 37396 44067 (4hrs 30mins).

Beinn a' Chreachain from Beinn Achaladair

*Beinn Mhanach
(on the right)*

To descend, continue north then northeast along the ridge above the picturesque Lochan a' Chreachain until a shallow col is reached just before the unnamed minor top, Point 961 (959 on older maps). From here descend grassy slopes to the northwest, crossing the Allt Coire an Lochain about halfway down and, continuing northwest through long grass, head for a break in the trees at 35525 45865. Avoid the trees at either side of this break, as they are hemmed in by deer fencing. Just before the railway line is reached a path is joined and this is followed to the southwest until a bridge crosses the line. A clear path heads back from here along the Water of Tulla, crossing a small burn (that can be awkward at times) and later crossing the Allt Coire Achaladair at a ford. This is not usually difficult unless it is in full spate, in which case it might be prudent to do the route in the reverse direction.

Beinn Mhanach can also be climbed with these two hills by heading northeast from the col at the head of the Allt Coire Achalladair to the peaty col between the Auch Gleann and the Gleann Cailliche. From there head east to reach the western slopes of Beinn Mhanach, which are climbed to its summit at 37373 41132. Return the same way to the col at the southern end of Beinn Achalladair. During the stalking season, however, the landowners request that Beinn Mhanach is climbed only by the approach described below (Route 43) along the Auch Gleann.

ROUTE 43

Beinn Mhanach (953m)

Pronunciation: Bine Vannoch
Translation: Mountain of the Monks

Distance:	18km
Ascent:	770m
Time:	4hrs 50mins
Maps:	OS sheet 50; Explorer map 377; Area Map 4
Parking:	roadside on A82
Start:	from A82 follow the private track past Auch, under the viaduct
Hostel:	YHA Crianlarich; Independent Tyndrum
B&B/hotel:	Tyndrum
Camping:	Tyndrum
Access:	Invermearan Estate, tel: 01887 866245

To reach this hidden Munro it is necessary to go deep into the Auch Gleann, once the home of the Glenorchy Bard. Now the inner sanctuary of the glen is home only to a herd of Highland cattle.

Whilst Beinn Mhanach can be climbed with Beinn Achaladair from the west (see Route 42), the estate owners are trying to persuade people to use the Auch Gleann approach to this rather undistinguished hill during the stalking season. There is very inadequate parking alongside the A82 close to the start of the private track along the glen. A larger parking area lies some distance along the main road to the northwest at 30959 36462.

Follow the track past the cottages at Auch and continue under the viaduct for some 7km. It should be possible to cycle for most of the way along this track, although some sections are quite rough.

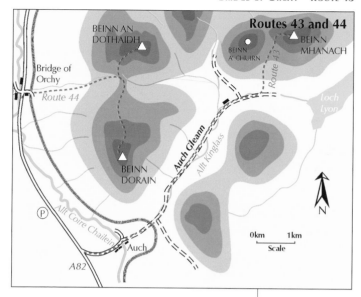

The track crosses the Allt Coire Chailein at a ford just beyond the buildings, and it also fords the Allt Kinglass six or seven times as it winds up the valley. In spate some of these crossings can be difficult without getting your feet wet. At the head of the glen take the right branch of the track where it divides and, shortly after this, take to the steep open hillside. A rising traverse can be made towards the col between the two domed summits of Beinn a' Chuirn and Beinn Mhanach. The ground is steep and pathless, but grassy throughout and without real difficulty. Continue up the final gentler summit slopes of **Beinn Mhanach** to its summit cairn at 37373 41132. This summit offers the best view of Beinn Dorain (3hrs).

Return by the route of ascent.

ROUTE 44

Beinn Dorain (1076m),

Beinn an Dothaidh (1004m)

Pronunciation: *Bine Doe-erenn; Bine uh Naw-hee*
Translation: *Mountain of the*
Little Gullies; Mountain of Scorching

Distance:	13½km
Ascent:	1210m
Time:	5hrs
Maps:	OS sheet 50; Explorer map 377; Area Map 4; see Route 43 for sketch map
Parking:	walkers' car park next to the Bridge of Orchy Hotel. Walkers are requested not to park at the station.
Start:	footpath from road goes under railway line
Hostel:	YHA Crianlarich; Independent bunkhouses at Bridge of Orchy and Tyndrum
B&B/hotel:	Bridge of Orchy; Tyndrum
Camping:	Tyndrum
Access:	tel: 01838 400233

The conical 'sand-castle' profiles of these two hills when seen from the west will be familiar to anyone who has driven along the A82. It is hard to make a circuit out of these hills, but the walk described here is a popular outing from Bridge of Orchy, despite having to retrace your steps on the return leg.

From the hotel go up to the station, and pass under the railway line and through a gate which leads onto the hill. The path is obvious, passing round an enclosed area where there is a radio mast and heading almost due east up the hill alongside the Allt Coire an Dothaidh. Higher up the corrie this burn tumbles over a small crag. It is crossed a couple of hundred metres below the crag, and

The celebrated poet Duncan MacIntyre – known as the Glenorchy Bard – lived for many years on the craggier and less well-known eastern side of these hills, in the Auch Gleann. Images of Beinn Dorain in particular feature strongly in his poems. To him this was the most beautiful of Scottish mountains.

> Precedence over other bens has Beinn Dobhrain.
>
> Of all I have seen beneath the sun I deemed her loveliest:
>
> A long unbroken moor; covert where deer are found;
>
> The brightness of the slope . . .

There is a track along the Auch Gleann from where an ascent of the eastern side can be made, but most people choose Bridge of Orchy as the starting point for their ascent, and the well-trodden trail up the western side of the hill is a pleasant but fairly easy outing which may leave the impression that Duncan's sentiments were excessive, if not altogether misplaced.

the path then does a small detour before arriving at the col where there is a cairn. Turn right (south) over slabby rocks and climb the ridge to reach a flat grassy area which is crossed. A little lochan is passed on the way

The Auch Gleann (Beinn Dorain on right) from Beinn Mhanach

Beinn Dorain (right) and Beinn an Dothaidh (left) from Bridge of Orchy

before you climb a stony path where the ridge rises again. A small secondary path leads off to the right and traverses somewhat needlessly below the top of the ridge to emerge just below the main summit. Keep to the main path on the crest, however, and you soon come to a large cairn at 32508 38212. Despite the size of this cairn it is not the highest point. Continue down and then up again for a few hundred metres to reach the true summit of **Beinn Dorain** at 32552 37849 (2hrs 45mins).

Retrace your steps to the col and follow the path to Beinn an Dothaidh over wet meadows. The path starts off purposefully but is hard to find after a few hundred metres, and a bearing may be needed to bring you to the correct top. There are only a few metres difference between the three tops along **Beinn an Dothaidh**'s curving ridge, and it is not at all clear from below which is the summit. In fact it is the middle top at 33180 40862 (4hrs). If you decide to visit the west top to take in the views, it would be best to descend from there a short way to the southeast initially and then return via your ascent path to the summit – a direct line down from the west top to the col would take you over crags.

Retrace your steps to the col and return the same way to the car park.

CRUACHAN

ROUTE 45

Ben Cruachan (1126m),
Stob Diamh (998m)

Pronunciation: *Ben Krooerchan; Stob Dive*
Translation: *Conical Heap on the Mountain; Peak of the Stag*

Distance:	13km
Ascent:	1320m
Time:	5hrs 40mins
Maps:	OS sheet 50; Explorer map 377; Area Map 4
Parking:	roadside on A85 by path to station (and a small power station)
Start:	footpath to bridge under railway line and up through woods
Hostel:	YHA Oban or Crianlarich; Independent Oban
B&B/hotel:	Lochawe
Camping:	Bridge of Awe; Tyndrum
Access:	tel: 01838 200638

The hills to the north of Lochawe offer two fine circuits for the hillwalker. One is the Dalmally horseshoe, which climbs Stob Diamh by the ridges around the glaciated valley of the Allt Coire Chreachainn. The other, the Cruachan horseshoe described here, climbs the ridges around the head of the Cruachan Reservoir, taking in two Munros: Ben Cruachan and Stob Diamh.

Starting from the A85 just east of the visitor centre, pass under the railway line at a small station and follow the path up through a native woodland, staying on the right of the burn. Climb a ladder onto the dam at its left-hand end and continue along the track on the west bank of the Cruachan Reservoir for 1½km. At the northern end of the

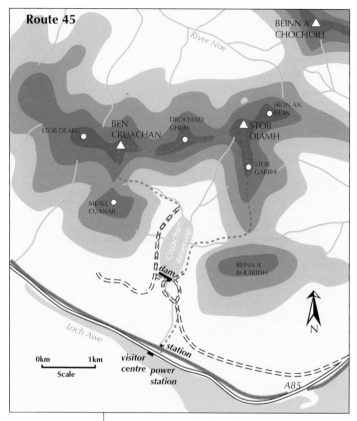

Route 45

BEINN A'
CHOCHUILL

River Noe

SRON AN
ISEAN

STOB DEARG

BEN
CRUACHAN

DROCHAID
GHLAS

STOB
DIAMH

STOB
GARBH

MEALL
CUANAIL

Cruachan
Reservoir

dam

BEINN A'
BHUIRIDH

N

Loch Awe

station

0km   1km

Scale

visitor
centre power
station

A85

reservoir a cairn marks the start of a footpath which leads up into Coire Dearg. Climb to the col between Meall Cuanail and Ben Cruachan and from here head north up through a jumble of boulders and stones to arrive somewhat suddenly at the summit of **Ben Cruachan** (06967 30463) (3hrs 5mins).

The ridge continues, dropping to the northeast. Clamber down over rocks and after a short distance bear east, taking care that you don't stray onto Cruachan's north ridge. Cross some inclined granite slabs and, staying close to the crest, work your way along the ridge, which is quite rocky in places but never difficult. The trail leads to the summit of Drochaid Ghlas (1009m). Go to this summit for the view, but return a short distance from here to a cairn which marks the continuation to Stob Diamh. If you try to descend directly from the summit of Drochaid Ghlas you are likely to end up either on its north ridge (and in trouble) or on steep rocks to the east (and still in trouble). From the cairn the path drops to the southeast then turns back to the east and climbs through more large stones to the summit cairn of **Stob Diamh** at 09481 30842 (4hrs 30mins).

To descend, head due south. This part of the route is shared with part of the Dalmally horseshoe. Pass over a minor top – Point 980 at 09561 30239 – and a few hundred metres beyond it bear off to the right through bouldery ground down a clearly defined ridge to the south. Drop down almost to the end of this ridge, until just before it begins to rise again to Beinn a' Bhuiridh, then head west down easy grassy slopes alongside the small burn that leads to the reservoir. From the dam, return by the route of ascent.

ROUTE 46

Beinn a' Chochuill (980m),

Beinn Eunaich (989m)

Pronunciation: Bine yuh Chochell; Bine Eh-neech
Translation: Cowled or Hooded Hill; Fowling Mountain

This shapely pair of hills to the east of Ben Cruachan offer pleasant walking and fine views over Stob Diamh and the Dalmally Horseshoe.

From the road go along the private track that takes you behind Castles Farm and high into the valley of the Allt

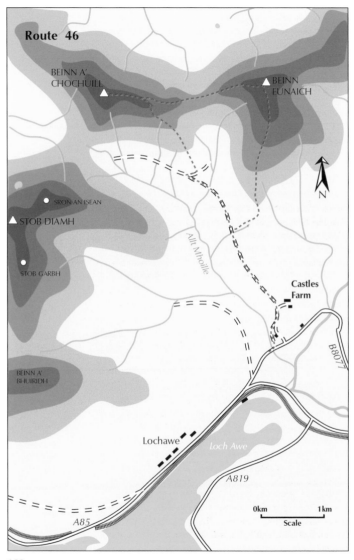

Distance:	14½km
Ascent:	1180m
Time:	5hrs 10mins
Maps:	OS sheet 50; Explorer map 377; Area Map 4
Parking:	limited parking where the road widens by the bridge over the Allt Mhoille on the B8077
Start:	along private track that bypasses Castles Farm
Hostel:	YHA Oban or Crianlarich; Independent Tyndrum or Oban
B&B/hotel:	Lochawe
Camping:	A85 southeast of Taynuilt
Access:	tel: 01838 200636

Mhoille. Stay on the track as it climbs quite steeply beneath Stob Maol. Shortly after it crosses the Allt Lairig Ianachain another track leads off to the right. Follow this for a couple of hundred metres to the point where it turns around the nose of Beinn a' Chochuill's southeast ridge and here take to the open hillside. The ridge is followed to the top, staying close to its crest all the way. A path, indistinct at first, soon appears, though it vanishes again close to the top. Once the main ridge is gained a well-trodden path leads pleasantly over stones and grass along the crest of quite a narrow ridge for nearly 1km until the summit cairn of **Beinn a' Chochuill** is reached at 10977 32832 (2hrs 50mins).

Return along the ridge and continue east-northeast, dropping down to the col between the two hills. The curving west ridge of **Beinn Eunaich** is stony and rocky and fairly steep higher up; however, there are no difficulties en route. Climb it to the top at 13564 32787 (4hrs 5mins).

From here it is an easy descent for 2km down the long, grassy south ridge. Go nearly to its end, but at 13286 30947 follow the path west-southwest where it plummets down steep, grassy slopes before finding a little rib to return you to the private track. (If you continue over the southern nose of Stob Maol there are crags as well as steep ground to be negotiated.) There is a small cairn on the track at 13015 30669 marking the point where the descent path comes down.

TYNDRUM

ROUTE 47

*Ben Lui (1130m), Beinn a' Chleibh (916m),
Ben Oss (1029m), Beinn Dubhchraig (978m)*

Pronunciation: *Ben Looee;
Bine yuh Chlayv; Ben Oss; Bine Doochreck*
Translation: *Mountain of the Calf;
Creel Hill; Elk Mountain; Mountain of the Dark Crag*

Distance:	25km
Ascent:	1730m
Time:	8hrs 30mins
Difficulty:	A long, demanding route which could be split into a number of easier options. Some mild exposure on Ben Lui's northeast ridge. If approaching from A85 a difficult river crossing is involved – may not be possible after heavy rainfall.
Maps:	OS sheet 50; Explorer map 364; Harvey's Superwalker map Crianlarich; Area Map 5
Parking:	car park off the A82 at Dalrigh
Start:	along private track to Cononish from north end of car park
Hostel:	YHA Crianlarich; Independent Tyndrum
B&B/hotel:	Tyndrum
Camping:	Tyndrum
Access:	Scottish Natural Heritage, tel: 01786 450362. Much of the route described also crosses privately owned land, but there should not be a conflict with other users if you adhere to this route. The area to the south of Ben Oss is part of the Glen Falloch Estate, tel: 01301 704229.

Starting from the car park at Dalrigh, just off the A82, walk back a few metres towards the road and take the private track past houses to the farm at Cononish. When

The range of hills to the southwest of Tyndrum has been scarred in places by commercial mining operations, mostly for gold. To the hillwalker, however, the Munros and ridges in this distinguished group are a gold mine of a different sort. Various routes and combinations are possible on these hills. The lovely Ben Lui dominates the group both in height and appearance, but the other three Munros have their own particular attractions. They are linked by a snaking ridge that varies considerably in character along its length: from the broad grassy saddle of Beinn a' Chleibh to the rough, rocky buttresses on the southern side of Ben Oss and the stony spine of Beinn Dubhchraig.

These hills can be picked off in ones and twos either from the A85 in the west or from Dalrigh, but to savour the real character of the group only a complete traverse does them full justice. This can be achieved from either starting point. Starting from the car park just off the A85, it is possible to cross the River Lochy at 23821 26603 and the railway line, climb up the Fionn Choirein and then, after completing the ridge, descend to Dalrigh at the end of the day. There are a number of problems with this, however. For a start two vehicles are required (or perhaps a co-operative non-hillwalking driver). Secondly Ben Lui's finest feature – its steep northeast ridge – is missed out altogether. And finally, crossing the River Lochy is rarely easy; it is a substantial river with no helpful stepping-stones across it. Furthermore the path beyond the river through the trees can be exceptionally boggy. For these reasons the route described here is a little longer and tougher, but offers an excellent day's hillwalking, full of interest, which combines the best of all four hills.

you have passed this eyesore and the mess of the old gold mine above it, Ben Lui takes centre stage. Continue on the track as far as it goes then cross the Allt an Rund and climb quite steeply alongside the Allt Coire Gaothach into the corrie. Once you are in the corrie head northwest up grassy slopes to gain the main ridge. Many people continue to the back of the corrie and climb the eroded scree slope to join the ridge higher up, but it is a less pleasant ascent. Once on the rocky ridge the route is always clear. It is quite steep in places and at times it narrows. Here and there you might use a hand, but no

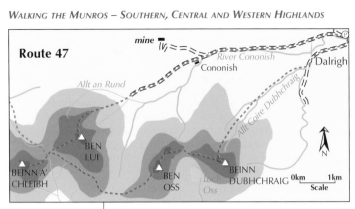

real scrambling is called for. There are occasional glimpses of the big drop into the Coire Gaothach but it is not an intimidating path (except perhaps in a high wind). There is a cairn at the top of the path but **Ben Lui**'s summit is a couple of hundred metres to its southeast at a second cairn (26637 26291) (3hrs 25mins).

Return to the midway point between the two cairns and descend west-southwest over boulders to the col, then continue easily up the broad grassy shoulder to the summit of **Beinn a' Chleibh** at 25056 25605 (4hrs 10mins).

Fortunately there is no need to reascend Ben Lui from here. Return to the col and continue uphill for 200–300m, then skirt around the mountain's south-western flanks, taking the easiest line and staying roughly along the same contour. The slope is grassy and not very steep, with occasional spillages of easy stones to cross. There is a wild and remote tract of moorland below you to the southwest. Eventually this line should bring you just above the wide col at the head of the Allt Coire Laoigh. There is a shy and rather elusive path through the numerous hillocks and moraines that cover the col. Escape is possible down this corrie to the northeast and will bring you back to Cononish, but the delight of Ben Oss ahead of you is not to be missed. Ben Oss is a rugged, complex hill with many rocky knolls and stone-covered slopes. Maybe it is not the easiest hill to find your way around in poor weather, and on its southern slopes at least the path is a luxury available only occasionally, but it has a sense of remoteness and rugged grandeur that many higher hills can't offer. The summit cairn is reached on **Ben Oss**'s stony dome at 28765 25339 (6hrs 5mins).

Continue north-northeast to a secondary top, then down over a series of rocky knolls to the Bealach Buidhe (the main path from the secondary top to the bealach takes a devious line further south). From the col the summit of **Beinn Dubhchraig** lies to the east-southeast and is reached by a broad stony ridge. There is a flattish step in the ridge where a number of little lochans nestle. Pass these and continue easily to the top at 30767 25495 (6hrs 55mins).

To descend, return almost to the little lochans and head north-northeast straight down the grassy slope. A path appears just to the left of the main burn and this leads eventually over three stiles that cross deer fencing. (At the time of writing two of the stiles had almost disintegrated.) The path also leads through some horrendous bogs; this is a shame because they severely detract from one's appreciation of the old Scots pines here – these lovely native trees are a rare remnant of the ancient Caledonian Pine Forest and they are extremely beautiful. Eventually a footbridge takes you over the burn and quickly leads to a private track; this crosses both the railway and then the River Cononish to bring you back to the car park.

Ben Lui, Ben Oss and Ben Dubhchraig from Ben Vane

GLEN LYON

ROUTE 48
Meall Buidhe (932m)

Pronunciation: *Miaowl Vooyer*
Translation: *Yellow Hill*

Distance:	9km
Ascent:	520m
Time:	3hrs 5mins
Maps:	OS sheet 51; Explorer map 378; Area Map 4
Parking:	roadside at 51210 46391
Start:	north up hill track that starts just east of the dam
Hostel:	YHA Killin
B&B/hotel:	Fearnan; Fortingall; Tummel Bridge; Killin
Camping:	Kenmore; Glengoulandie; A827 NE of Killin
Access:	Lochs Estate, tel: 01887 866224

Dams have been constructed across two of the valleys at the western end of Glen Lyon to create reservoirs. Loch an Daimh, the northern one of these, lies just to the north of the main glen and stretches between two fairly easy Munros, Meall Buidhe and Stuchd an Lochain, which are often climbed together.

Meall Buidhe, to the north of Loch an Daimh, can be approached from the western end of Loch Rannoch, but the shortest and most straightforward approach to this hill is from the head of the valley, as described here, starting just below the dam of Loch an Daimh. Park at a widening in the road to the east of the dam. From here **Meall Buidhe** can easily be climbed, along with Stuchd an Lochain, in a single day.

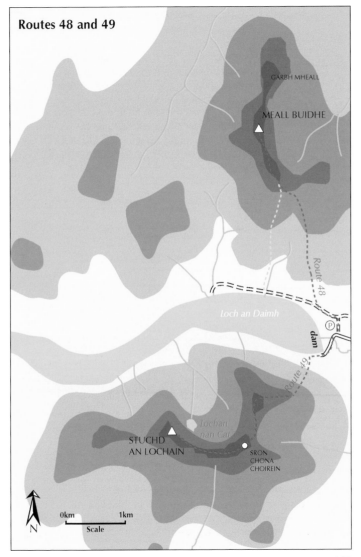

Routes 48 and 49

GARBH MHEALL

MEALL BUIDHE

Route 48

Loch an Daimh

dam

Route 49

Lochan nan Cat

STUCHD
AN LOCHAIN

SRON
CHONA
CHOIREIN

0km   1km
Scale

N

A rough track leads up from the road for 250m. Follow the track until it branches, then leave it for a path that leads north onto the open hillside. The path climbs steadily north, then northwest, until it reaches the southern end of the summit ridge. The ridge is quite broad and gives easy walking past a minor top to the summit cairn at 49840 49940 (1hr 50mins).

In descent the same route can be followed back to the cars or, for a little variety, a line can be taken to the loch by descending on the western side of the Coire nam Miseach. From there return by the track along the eastern edge of the loch.

ROUTE 49

Stuchd an Lochain (960m)

Pronunciation: Stook an Lochan
Translation: Steep Conical Hill of the Lochan

Distance:	9km
Ascent:	600m
Time:	2hrs 55mins
Maps:	OS sheet 51; Explorer map 378; Area Map 4; see Route 48 for sketch map
Parking:	at the foot of the dam
Start:	track to south east side of dam, then path up hillside
Hostel:	YHA Killin
B&B/hotel:	Fearnan; Fortingall; Tummel Bridge; Killin
Camping:	Kenmore; Glengoulandie; A827 NE of Killin
Access:	(if climbed from the dam) Lochs Estate, tel: 01887 866224

There doesn't seem to be enough climbing for this hill or its neighbour, Meall Buidhe, to be fully-fledged Munros, but that's because the road takes you to a height of over 400m before the car has to be left.

East ridge of Stuchd an Lochain from the summit

Walk beneath the dam to its southeast end. A short distance along the side of the loch a path leads onto the hill. At first it goes gently along the hillside, then faces the slope head-on and climbs directly up to the ridge, emerging below the minor top of Creag an Fheadain. From this point on there is a line of old rusting fence posts, quite close together, that leads all the way to the small summit cairn of **Stuchd an Lochain**. Follow the posts over Creag an Fheadain, down 40m or so into a little dip, then easily over Sron Chona Choirein and gently around a long curving ridge above the Lochan nan Cat to the final short steep section to the summit at 48306 44834 (2hrs).

Return by the same route. The only possibility of a route-finding error on this route is to miss the descent path from the ridge to the dam, but even this is marked by a small cairn (though it is not quite big enough to be regarded as a permanent fixture).

ROUTE 50

Carn Gorm (1029m), Meall Garbh (968m),

Carn Mairg (1042m), Meall na Aighean

(Creag Mhor) (981m)

Pronunciation: *Karn Gorrum; Miaowl*
Garav; Karn Merrick; Miaowl nun ion; Krayk Voar
Translation: *Blue Hill; Rough Hill; Red or Rusty Hill; Big Crag*

Distance:	18km
Ascent:	1340m
Time:	6hrs 30mins
Maps:	OS sheet 51; Explorer map 378; Area Map 4
Parking:	limited roadside parking in Invervar; there is a small parking area just at the start of the private road to Dericambus
Start:	footpath through metal gate almost opposite phone box
Hostel:	YHA Killin
B&B/hotel:	Fortingall; Fearnan; Killin
Camping:	Kenmore; Glengoulandie; A827 north west of Killin
Access:	North Chesthill Estate, tel: 01887 877207 or 01887 829245. The estate requests that dogs are not taken on this walk. Ring for information if doing this route during the stalking season.

This group of four makes an excellent circuit when approached from Glen Lyon, with fine scenery and good walking throughout.

The walk starts in Invervar on the north side of the road at a metal gate, which is festooned with instructions, and which lies between the small private Dericambus road and a public phone box. Pass through the metal gate and follow the track through trees. The track passes through a couple of gates before emerging from the trees. For about 1½km it runs alongside the Invervar

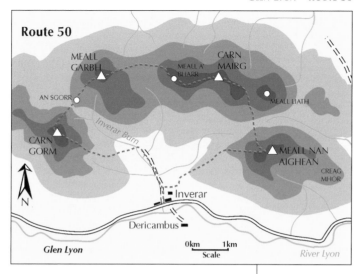

The circuit of these hills from Glen Lyon is reminiscent in some respects of the circuit from Sgairneach Mhor to Geal Charn by the Drumochter Pass (Route 16). The feel of the walking is very similar. Both areas have the same grassy, rolling outlines with longish walks between the tops, a similar surface geology of quartzose mica schist and quartz feldspar, and the same cover of clipped grass with stretches of peat and heather and occasional scree and boulder fields near the tops. They are both important areas for deer. The eighteenth-century poet Duncan MacIntyre, known as the Glenorchy Bard, wrote a poem in praise of Creag Mhor called 'Coire a' Cheathaich' ('corrie of the mists'): '... Lovely is the coat of Creag Mhor'.

Burn, crossing a tributary burn, the Allt Coire a' Chearcaill, and continues past another tributary burn at the top of the treeline. At this point cross the Invervar Burn, climbing its steep west bank, then head southwest on a rising path that climbs the southeast ridge of **Carn Gorm**. This path veers gradually round to the northwest as it climbs steadily upwards, passing over a couple of false tops before it reaches the summit cairn at 63479 50134 (2hrs 15mins).

From the summit, drop quite steeply at first to the northeast, towards Meall Garbh. The path bypasses the minor top of An Sgorr, but this can easily be included if desired. The route up the bouldery final slopes of Meall Garbh is marked by a line of old fence posts. Indeed the summit cairn of **Meall Garbh** is built mostly of old metal fence posts 64694 51686 (2hrs 55mins).

The fence posts continue to mark the line of descent to a small lochan, bypassing the southeastern top of Meall Garbh. The ridge undulates from here for the next 3km to Carn Mairg, with a couple of small cairns at 66663 51855 and 67361 51631, but the fence posts can be followed the whole way. Climb quite steeply over Meall a' Bharr before dropping to a little col below the north top of **Carn Mairg**. Continue up to this top and when the summit rocks are reached turn abruptly to the right (southeast) and continue over boulders to the higher south top and the summit cairn at 68493 51255 (4hrs 20mins).

From the summit descend to the east down bouldery scree, passing to the left (north) of a small crag. Continue east to a col between Carn Mairg and Meall Liath, and skirt for a short distance around Meall Liath before picking up the broad ridge that leads towards Creag Mhor. The next summit you are heading for is marked Meall na Aighean on the current OS map, though it does not appear on some older maps. (Confusingly Craig Mhor is shown on modern

Carn Gorm from
Meall Garbh

maps as being the name for the crags above Coille Dhubh, some 3km to the southeast of the main top and well away from your route. Historically, however, and on older OS maps, it is the name of the mountain as a whole.) A well-trodden path leads onto the northern flanks of Meall na Aighean, but it arrives nearer the southwest top than the higher northeast top. When the summit ridge is reached turn to the northeast to reach the rocky top of **Meall na Aighean** at 69478 49656 (5hrs 20mins).

The descent to Invervar lies along the mountain's west ridge, which is almost due west of the last summit. Traverse past the southwest top. At first the ridge is broad and in mist it is indistinct, but it soon narrows to become more clearly defined. Stay on the crest along its entire length and drop gradually down to join the path along the Invervar Burn, which takes you back to the road.

ROUTE 51

Schiehallion (1083m)

Pronunciation: *Sheehallion*
Translation: *The Fairy Hill of the Caledonians*

Distance:	9km
Ascent:	750m
Time:	3hrs 45mins
Maps:	OS sheet 52; Explorer map 386; Area Map 4
Parking:	car park at Braes of Foss (but limited spaces)
Start:	path from the south end of the car park
Hostel:	YHA, Killin, Pitlochry
B&B/hotel:	Tummel Bridge, Aberfeldy
Camping:	Glengoulandie (B846)
Access:	Braes of Foss Farm, tel: 01887830324. Make sure you avoid the old path in descent.

Schiehallion is a lovely hill and, despite the obvious problems that arise from large visitor numbers, the long east ridge has a certain allure that always endures.

Poor old Schiehallion. A victim of its beautiful name and handsome profile, visible from hill-tops all over the southern Highlands. Thousands of boots tramp up and down it each year, and the consequent erosion is severe in places. The new owners of the eastern side of the hill – the John Muir Trust – are trying hard to improve things. They have changed the line of the path at the bottom of the hill, upgraded the car park and are attempting to combat the effects of erosion.

As well as being a hill of beauty this is also a hill of science as a plaque by the car park entrance reminds us. Nevil Meskalyne set up an experiment here with plumb lines in observatories on either side of the mountain to test whether the mass of the mountain would have an effect on gravitational pull. The mathematician who helped with the measurements for this experiment was Charles Hutton who, as part of his work, drew contour lines to describe the shape of the hill. This was the very first use of contour lines, which are now used universally in mapping throughout the world.

Still on a scientific note, Schiehallion offers the ultimate proof of Cairn's law. Cairn's law, of course, states that 'mountain cairns multiply in direct proportion to the number of available stones to build them'. On the broad east ridge of Schiehallion there are huge numbers of stones and ... lo and behold, huge numbers of cairns as well. In future years one can imagine them being linked up to become an unbroken wall of stones guiding the way. Fortunately the John Muir Trust has plans to remove some of the cairns in future, leaving only the ones that are of historical significance.

From the car park follow the new path to the hill. The old route (marked on OS maps prior to 2004) passed to the north of the small plantation of trees, then followed a boggy, eroded trail until it gave way to stones and veered round to the west. The new path (opened in 2004) gains the main ridge further east, to the south of the plantation, and has been carefully laid so that the encounter with long stretches of eroded grass and bog in the lower reaches of the hill will hopefully now be a thing of the past.

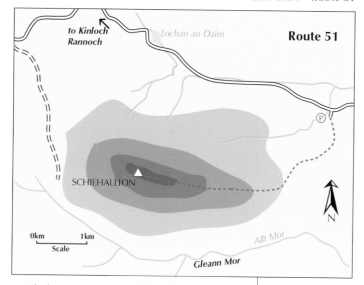

The long central section of the ridge rises slowly and is fairly featureless in mist – except for those cairns. The walking is quite rough over the lumpy carpet of quartzite stones. The ridge narrows further up, until the path reaches **Schiehallion**'s rocky summit capped by a surprisingly modest cairn (considering what has gone before) at 71374 54757 (2hrs 15mins).

Return by the same route.

Schiehallion from the summit of Sgor Gaibhre

GLEN LOCHAY

ROUTE 52
Creag Mhor (1047m),
Beinn Heasgarnich (1078m)

Pronunciation: Krayk Voar; Bine Heskarnich
Translation: Big Cliff; Sheltering Mountain

Distance:	21km
Ascent:	1290m
Time:	7hrs 15mins
Maps:	OS sheet 50 and 51; Explorer map 378; Area Map 4
Parking:	at start of private track just beyond Kenknock in Glen Lochay
Start:	along private track that heads west into Glen Lochay
Hostel:	YHA Killin
B&B/hotel:	Killin
Camping:	A827 north of Killin
Access:	Glen Lochay farm manager, tel: 01567 820553

These two big hills, tucked away at the far end of Glen Lochay, are well guarded by the surrounding hills. Creag Mhor is perhaps the more straight-forward of the two, but Beinn Heasgarnich is set in a wild tract of countryside and hides behind Stob an Fhir Bhogha to the south. To the east it is guarded by some rough peat moorland interspersed with numerous rocky outcrops. The road in Glen Lochay offers the only obvious approach.

Just beyond Kenknock Farm is a crossroads: a forestry road leads south to reach a small plantation across the River Lochay and a narrow road climbs north over the pass to Glen Lyon. There is room here to park several cars. Continue on foot along the private track that wanders alongside the river past Badour to Batavaime. Climb up

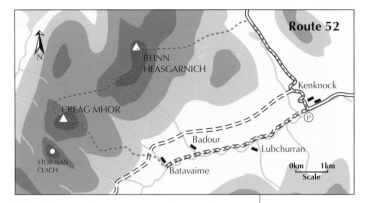

behind the croft to the northwest onto the nose of Sron nan Eun, the southeast ridge of Creag Mhor. The easiest line through the crags can clearly be seen as you approach: it follows a grassy traverse to the west beneath the first crags, then climbs quite steeply through boulders back to the right and finally heads back to the northwest to gain the easy upper part of the ridge. From here the path along the ridge is fairly clear, climbing steadily along the crest to **Creag Mhor**'s summit cairn at 39157 36108 (3hrs 20mins).

Creag Mhor's eastern and northeastern faces are steep and craggy. To proceed safely to Beinn Heasgarnich it is necessary to descend some way down the northwest ridge of Creag Mhor until the crags have been cleared. From the summit, first head west-northwest, then northwest for a few hundred metres (to 38740 36380), until it is safe to descend east down easy grassy slopes to reach the peaty col below Stob an Fhir-Bhogha's west ridge. Climb the ridge quite steeply to the cairned top at 41143 37227, then continue over a hummocky section for 1½km to reach **Beinn Heasgarnich**'s summit cairn at 41382 38332 (5hrs 20mins).

There are two or three options for descent. Perhaps the quickest is to return to Stob an Fhir-Bhogha then drop south quite steeply at first to regain the private track. There is some very steep ground beneath this top, and to avoid the worst of this it is best to start this descent just

Creag Mhor from Stob an Fhir-bhoga (Beinn Heasgarnich)

to the west of the summit, where the angle is a little easier. Descent can also be made by returning all the way to the col and then following the Allt Batavaim back to the track. A third option is to descend directly to the east from the summit of Beinn Heasgarnich. This is certainly the most interesting way back, although it takes you into some very rough and rather wet terrain, with a number of unexpectedly steep sections and a couple of waterfalls to avoid. The area around (and especially to the south of) the Lochan Achlarich is riven with peat hags, and the easiest line is to pass around the northern end of Creag nam Bodach to reach the tarmac road that links Glen Lyon with Glen Lochay. Return from here along the road.

ROUTE 53

Ben Challum (1025m)

Pronunciation: *Ben Challum*
Translation: *Malcolm's Mountain*

At the head of Glen Lochay lies a fine, shapely peak that is not often climbed from this side. The more usual approach to Ben Challum is from the A82 south of Tyndrum, but the approach along the length of Glen Lochay is surely more pleasant, taking the walker beneath the brooding forms of several Munros en route to its steep, pathless east ridge.

Cars should be left in the clearing at Kenknock, just before the road turns to climb over a high pass to Glen Lyon. Walk along the private track, passing the old crofts at Badour and Batavaime (now a mountaineering club hut), until it veers round directly beneath Ben Challum's east ridge. Older maps don't show this track beyond Batavaime, but in fact it continues high up onto the western flanks of Meall Glas. Immediately after you have crossed the Allt Challum, by some corrugated sheep pens at 41273 33577, leave the track and gain height gradually

Distance:	21km
Ascent:	830m
Time:	6hrs 30mins (5hrs if a bike is used on the track)
Maps:	OS sheets 50 and 51; Explorer map 378; Area Map 4
Parking:	Kenknock at start of private track
Start:	along private track that leads west into Glen Lochay
Hostel:	YHA Killin
B&B/hotel:	Killin
Camping:	A827 north of Killin
Access:	Glen Lochay farm manager, tel: 01567 820553

over grassy hills, staying close to the right-hand side of the ridge. At about half-height a rocky outcrop is passed on its left. From here a little ramp (with a ribbon of scree on it) leads back right to the crest of the ridge above the crag.

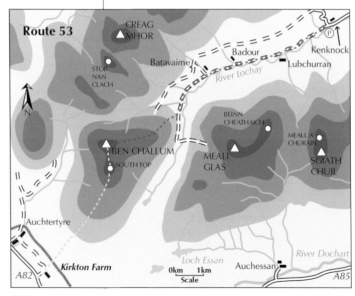

After a further 100m the angle eases off and the ridge continues easily for just over 1km over a mossy humpback until the final climb to **Ben Challum**'s summit. This last little section is fairly steep – but thankfully not nearly as steep as it appears from Glen Lochay – though without difficulty. Climb to the large summit cairn at 38683 32230 (4hrs; 45 minutes less if a bike is used along the track).

Return by the same route. If descending in poor visibility, care needs to be taken with navigation as the profile of the ridge is quite rounded with no obvious markers. Head for GR 39896 32474, which is the point at the top of the steep lower section. Stay to the left (north) of rocks here until you pass back to the right down the little ramp. Beyond this there should be no further difficulties.

Ben Challum from the east ridge

ROUTE 54

Meall Glas (959m), Sgiath Chuil (921m)

Pronunciation: *Miaowl Glaz; Skeer Hool*
Translation: *Grey-green Hill; Back Wing or Sheltering Place*

Distance:	18km
Ascent:	1220m
Time:	6hrs 25mins
Maps:	OS sheet 51; Explorer map 378; Area Map 4
Parking:	parking area on corner beyond the farm at Kenknock
Start:	along private track that leads west into Glen Lochay
Hostel:	YHA Killin
B&B/hotel:	Killin
Camping:	A827 north of Killin
Access:	Glen Lochay farm manager, tel: 01567 820553

The two Munros between Glen Lochay and Glen Dochart can be approached from either glen. Although they are only 3km apart and are usually climbed together, there is a considerable height loss between them and very steep slopes have to be negotiated on both sides of the gap, making this quite a tough walk. From the summit of Sgiath Chuil there are very fine views of Ben More and the Crianlarich hills.

Perhaps the most natural approach is from Glen Lochay, where a good circuit can be made starting at Kenknock and utilising the north ridges of both hills. There is no longer a bridge across the River Lochay at Lubchurran, but the river can be crossed just over 2km further upstream at Badour, where an old footbridge is still quite serviceable.

Walk along the track to Badour and cross the bridge, then head straight up the grassy hillside, making for the lowest

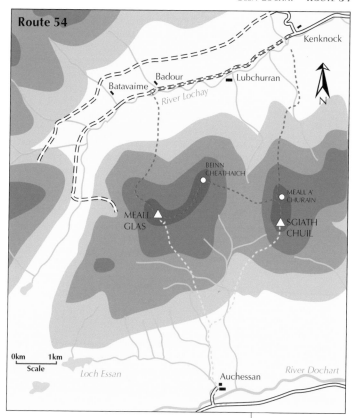

Route 54

Kenknock

Badour · Lubchurran

Batavaime

River Lochay

BEINN
CHEATHAICH

MEALL A'
CHURAIN

MEALL
GLAS

SGIATH
CHUIL

N

0km   1km
Scale

Loch Essan   Auchessan   River Dochart

point on the skyline. When height is gained in the high
corrie above, make for the ridge on the right. The going
becomes more stony and less steep once the ridge is
gained. Continue up to the summit cairn of **Meall Glas** at
43147 32189 (3hrs 15mins).

Drop quite sharply down to the east and follow a path
across the col to Beinn Cheathaich, bypassing Point 908
to its left. The east side of Beinn Cheathaich is peppered
with little crags so, to proceed to Sgiath Chuil, continue
past the trig point, dropping down to the north for about

100m until the ridge begins to level off, then descend steeply down the grassy slope to the east to reach the col between Cheathaich and Meall a' Churain. Pick a line through the peat hags and mires on the col then grit your teeth and climb up the steep grassy slope on the other side to arrive eventually on the wide ridge just north of **Sgiath Chuil**. Continue up to the summit cairn, which is a fine viewpoint, at 46294 31794 (5hrs 10mins).

To descend, follow the long north ridge of Sgiath Chuil for 2½km, crossing Meall a' Churain and dropping gradually until the last outlier on the ridge is reached, just beyond another area of peat hags. Turn right (northeast) around the foot of this hill and make for a small dam and footbridge over the Allt Innisdaimh at 46565 35250. If you're feeling hot after the day's exertions you may wish to take a dip in an excellent deep pool by the waterfall a few metres above the dam. Continue past trees to a gate that opens onto the forestry track and follow this back to Kenknock.

ROUTE 55

Meall Ghaordaidh (1039m)

Pronunciation: Miaowl Gurday
Translation: Hill of the Shoulder

Distance:	10km
Ascent:	930m
Time:	3hrs 35mins
Maps:	OS sheet 51; Explorer map 378; Area Map 4
Parking:	roadside just west of the Allt Dhuin Croisg at Duncroisk
Start:	through gated field on farm track
Hostel:	YHA Killin
B&B/hotel:	Killin
Camping:	A827 north of Killin
Access:	Boreland Estate, tel: 01567 820562

This straightforward hill is sufficiently isolated from the other Munros in this area that it has to be climbed on its own. It is useful to keep up one's sleeve as a bad-weather climb, or for one of those rare days when your enthusiasm for navigational epics has temporarily deserted you. That said, it is a fairly relentless slog up the long southeast ridge from Glen Lochay, which is the usual line of approach.

There is enough space for a few cars at a widening in the road to the west of the Allt Dhuin Croisg. From the road a rough farm track leads through the gated field and up past some stone ruins on the left until it reaches open

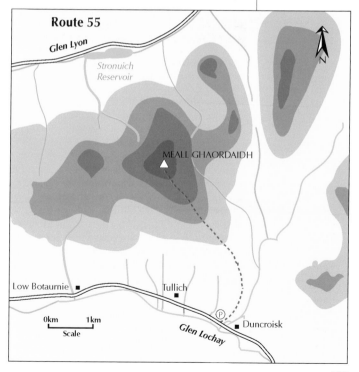

Route 55

Glen Lyon

Stronuich Reservoir

MEALL GHAORDAIDH

Low Botaurnie

Tullich

Duncroisk

Glen Lochay

0km   1km
Scale

N

Arriving on the summit of Meall Ghaordaidh

ground. Continue on the track, which runs parallel to the burn, until some old shielings are reached above the tree line. Here turn up the broad grassy ridge and head north-northwest all the way to the top. A single metal pole marks the way. A slightly more direct line can be taken starting from another single pole before the shielings are reached.

The route has a little more interest higher up as it weaves between some broken rocks. A good cairn enclosure at the top of **Meall Ghaordaidh** offers protection from the wind at 51449 39694 (2hrs 30mins).

The hill can be climbed more directly from further along the Glen Lochay road but there are no advantages in doing so. It can also be climbed from Stronuich in Glen Lyon – although few parties approach it from this side – by crossing the River Lyon at Stronuich and climbing steeply alongside the Allt Laoghain.

To return, descend by the same route.

ROUTE 56
Meall nan Tarmachan (1044m)

Pronunciation: Miaowl nun Tarmachan
Translation: Hill of the Ptarmigan

Distance:	12½km
Ascent:	840m
Time:	4hrs 35mins
Difficulty:	there is a short section of scrambling (grade 1) on the west side of Meall Garbh that has become awkward due to heavy erosion, but this section can be avoided altogether
Maps:	OS sheet 51; Explorer map 378; Harvey's Superwalker map Ben Lawers; Area Map 4
Parking:	at start of estate track, ½km north of the Ben Lawers Visitor Centre
Start:	along track southwest from parking area
Hostel:	YHA Killin
B&B/hotel:	Killin
Camping:	Milton Morenish on A827
Access:	National Trust for Scotland (if approached from the south). Visitor centre, tel: 01567 820397. Boreland Estate (if approached from the north), tel: 01567 820562

To the west of the Lawers ridge, on the other side of the minor road that leads to Glen Lyon, lies a group of hills having similar geology and botany, with an interesting connecting ridge and some impressive craggy faces. Whilst Meall nan Tarmachan is the only Munro in the group, and it can of course be climbed alone, few parties coming this far would not wish to complete the circuit along the whole ridge.

The usual approach is from a turning ½km north of the Lawers Visitor Centre. This offers the chance of a full circuit from Meall nan Tarmachan to Creag na Caillich. An alternative approach from the north is also possible, starting from the northwest of the Lochan na Lairige and walking around the great amphitheatre of Coire Riadhailt, starting up Meall Glas and Beinn a' Bhuic in the west and finishing along Tarmachan's north ridge, above Creag an Lochain in the east. Whilst this misses some of the main ridge, it is still a good outing and is increasing in popularity.

Since there are no grazing rights on the southern side of the Tarmachan range, a lot of the National Trust's ecological restoration work in this part of the Breadalbane Mountains has been concentrated here. Golden rod, wood cranesbill, bitter vetch, mountain sorrel and globeflower are amongst the many indigenous species that are now making a gradual comeback under this programme. It is hoped to regenerate the nationally rare woolly willow and to restore some of the montane willow scrub that once would have characterized this area.

Walk along the private track for a few hundred metres until an obvious, newly constructed path leads off to the right across the moor-side to the foot of Tarmachan's south ridge. Climb the grassy ridge along its crest. At Point 923 (GR 58929 38509) pass over a minor cairned top, then drop a short distance to a stile over an electrified fence. From here there is a short but steep climb up a little valley. The path here has been recently constructed by the National Trust for Scotland. The angle

The Tarmachan ridge – Beinn nan Eachan and Meall Garbh from Creag na Caillich

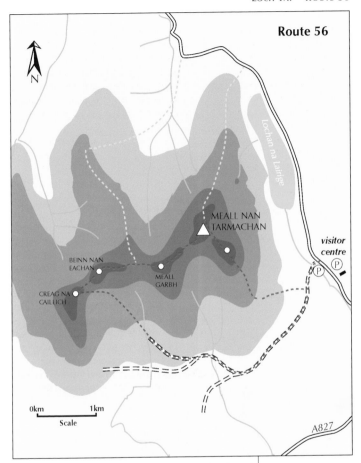

Route 56

eases higher up. Continue, with the summit heights of
Meall nan Tarmachan on your left, until a little col is
reached. At this point, double back for about 100m to the
summit cairn at 58526 38997 (1hr 45mins).

Leave to the southwest. There is a clear path along
the whole length of this ridge, which almost eliminates
route-finding problems for the summer walker. After a

short descent past a small lochan, pass two rather fancy cast-iron posts that mark the start of the ascent to Meall Garbh. There is no cairn to mark the summit of this hill at 57837 38334, but as soon as you have reached it the ridge narrows almost to a knife-edge for a short distance. Descend to a col beneath Beinn nan Eachan. This involves a steep scramble down some eroded, and in places quite polished, rock. There is no great difficulty here, but those who are intimidated by such pleasures will find a way to bypass the problems to the right (north), starting a little further back. Continue over a number of dips and rises to Beinn nan Eachan (very small cairn at 57026 38366) and then to Creag na Caillich. The first high point you arrive at on this last hill is the summit (no cairn) at 56285 37669 (3hrs 15mins).

Descend back along this last stretch to a small cairn on the col, then drop quite steeply over grass and take a bearing to GR 57309 37284 – the point where the private track doubles back on itself just before it reaches a small quarry. From here it is a simple walk back along the track to the start.

ROUTE 57

Beinn Ghlas (1103m), Ben Lawers (1214m),

An Stuc (1118m), Meall Garbh (1118m),

Meall Greigh (1001m)

Pronunciation: *Bine Glaz; Ben Lawers;*
Un Stook; Miaowl Garav; Miaowl Gree
Translation: *Grey-green Mountain; Mountain of*
the Hoof or Claw or, more likely, Loud Mountain;
Rocky Cone; Rough Hill; Hill of the Cattle Herd

There are a number of ways onto the ridge from both Glen Lyon in the north and Glen Tay in the south. The most obvious and the most popular is to start at the visitor centre car park on the Lochan na Lairige road above the

Distance:	16km to Lawers (21km if returning to Ben Lawers Visitor Centre)
Ascent:	1440m
Time:	6hrs 55mins (to Lawers)
Difficulty:	a short section of simple scrambling (up to grade1) on the northeast side of An Stuc
Maps:	OS sheet 51; Explorer map 378; Harvey's Superwalker map Ben Lawers; Area Map 4
Parking:	visitor centre car park
Start:	footpath from the car park at 80850 37950
Hostel:	YHA Killin
B&B/hotel:	Killin/Loch Tay
Camping:	there are several campsites on the A827 road between Killin and Lawers
Access:	with the exception of the last ½km of the route described, where the footpath passes through a private farm, all of the route is within the boundary of land owned by the National Trust for Scotland. Some areas fenced to protect wildlife. NTS, tel: 01567 820553. Visitor Centre, tel: 01567 820397

The traverse of the five peaks on the main Lawers ridge is a justifiably popular excursion that could be extended to include Meall a' Choire Leith and Meall Corranaich to make a long and fairly arduous traverse of the whole ridge. Most parties, however, will be happy to split the full ridge into two excellent walks as described here.

A827. The end of the day can be made easier if a car or bike is left in Lawers, although there are very few public parking spaces here.

From the car park a well-defined path climbs steadily up to the south ridge of Beinn Ghlas. For a time the path follows the Burn of Edramuchy through a conservation area which is fenced off to protect the fragile and rare ecology. After 1½km the path veers round to the northeast

The Breadalbane Mountains stretching from Ben Lui in the west to Ben Lawers in the east comprise one of the most important botanical regions in Scotland. The geology of easily weathered calcareous mica schists in these parts has created a fertile breeding ground for a large number of rare plants such as the alpine forget-me-not, drooping saxifrage, snow gentian, alpine bartsia and mountain bladder-fern. Unfortunately relentless overgrazing by sheep and deer (but more particularly by sheep) has led to the extinction of many species from the area and put many more under threat.

The National Trust for Scotland has purchased a large area including the Lawers/Tarmachan range and is putting a lot of effort into saving and restoring the special ecology of this area. Unfortunately, despite its new ownership, there are still grazing rights for sheep on the Lawers range, so most of the rarer plants here can only be found on ledges in high gullies which are fairly inaccessible. It goes without saying that wild plants should never be picked.

Many of the hills in the Ben Lawers range are grassy and fairly gentle in outline, with few of the rugged crags and exposed rocks that are found in other areas. Nonetheless there is plenty of variety and interest in the traverse described here. Owing to the proximity of the visitor centre, a large number of tourists make excursions into these hills in the summer months and there is a lot of erosion on the paths. Winter is probably the best time for a visit.

and divides. The left branch heads up the Coire Odhar to the col between Meall Corranaich and Beinn Ghlas. The right branch climbs more steeply along the ridge to the cairned summit of **Beinn Ghlas** at 62534 40456 (1hr 55mins).

From Beinn Ghlas drop down to the east and follow the broad ridge round until it climbs to the summit of **Ben Lawers** at 63552 41424 (2hrs 40mins).

Do not be confused by the ridge path that leads down to the southeast from the summit. This leads to the Lochan nan Cat and then back down to Lawers. Instead follow the continuation of the main ridge, which leads off to the north. This drops quite steeply for over ½km before rising slightly to cross the minor top Craig an Fhithich at 63570 42238. After another drop the path rises steeply again to reach the rocky ramparts of **An Stuc** at 63878 43094 (3hrs 35mins).

The descent from An Stuc to the northeast is the trickiest part of this route, involving a scramble (or a slide) down steep, loose, eroded rocks. There are a number of alternative lines with little to chose between them. Although the difficulties are short-lived and are not particularly exposed, care needs to be taken, especially in wet or icy weather. Don't come unstuck on An Stuc. From the little col just below the difficult section, the

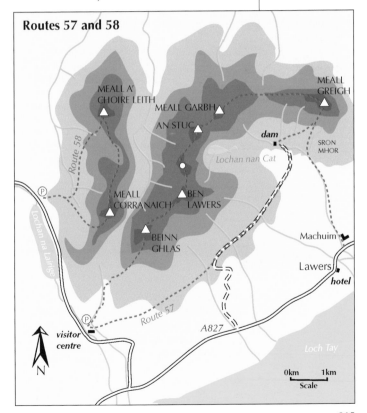

Routes 57 and 58

The Breadalbane Hills from Dochart Falls, Killin

route rises once more to reach the summit of **Meall Garbh** at 64439 43753 (4hrs 5mins).

From the summit the path heads northeast, following the line of a boundary fence. After nearly 1km this turns sharply to the southeast and it is followed down, eventually reaching a col. There is an easy descent from here to the shielings, where a track reaches a small dam on the Lawers Burn, although part of the hillside above the dam is enclosed by deer fencing to protect the flora. From the col at Point 65730 44009 continue in an easterly direction for 1½km. The broad grassy west ridge of **Meall Greigh** curves gently and rises gradually with a couple of undulations on a shoulder at 920m. Eventually a small cairn is reached at 67259 43931. This is a subsidiary top. To reach the summit proper continue on for a couple of hundred metres to a larger cairn at the southeastern end of the hill at 67401 43796 (5hrs 25mins).

To descend, take a bearing down easy grassy slopes to the Lawers Burn. A path then follows the burn, joining a more prominent path lower down, and after crossing a couple of stiles it passes through pleasant larch woodland to reach the road. Machuim farmyard is avoided by a small path to the right.

If traversing the hills back to the Ben Lawers Visitor Centre, take a bearing from the summit of Meall Greigh to the dam at 66198 42731 and follow the track until it doubles back and starts to descend just before reaching the Allt an Tuim Bhric. From here take to the hillside and follow the contours past a number of old shielings until the car park is reached. There is archaeological evidence of some old settlements around here, and a number of finds show that Mesolithic people visited these hills over 6000 years ago. Alongside Loch Tay there are also some crannogs.

ROUTE 58

Meall Corranaich (1069m),

Meall a' Choire Leith (926m)

Pronunciation: *Miaowl Korraneech; Miaowl uh Horrer Leer*
Translation: *Hill of the Sickle; Hill of the Grey Corrie*

Distance:	10km
Ascent:	750m
Time:	3hrs 30mins
Maps:	OS sheet 51; Explorer map 378; Harvey's Superwalker map Ben Lawers; Area Map 4; see Route 57 for sketch map
Parking:	by roadside just north of Lochan na Lairige beneath a prominent cairn
Start:	from roadside cairn across heather
Hostel:	YHA Killin
B&B/hotel:	Killin
Camping:	A827 north of Killin
Access:	Roro Estate, tel: 01887 877222 or 01887 866216

Head across heather to the upper reaches of the Allt Gleann Da Eig and follow this up the corrie to a line of old fence posts just below the crest of the west ridge of Meall Corranaich. A broken path also reaches this point from the

The two most westerly hills of the great Ben Lawers ridge offer a short but worthwhile circuit starting from the small cairned lay-by just north of the Lochan na Lairige. Starting from a height of 550m there is less climbing involved than for most Munros and this makes for a fairly short day.

broad enclosing ridge to the west of the burn. Continue up along the line of posts past a subsidiary cairn at 61461 40949 to **Meall Corranaich**'s true summit at 61534 41030.

From here follow the long curving ridge northwards for nearly 1km until it broadens out into a flat shoulder. At 61557 41867 head northeast to gain the narrower ridge that now leads north to the head of Coire Liath. (An obvious path at the head of Coire Gorm cuts off the corner and regains the ridge further along). Skirt around the crags that tumble into Coire Liath and then begin the climb to **Meall a' Choire Leith**. The summit cairn is in the middle of the wide grassy top at 61262 43897.

To descend, it is possible to head southwest straight down the grassy slopes of Meall a' Choire Leith. Cross the small tributary of the Allt Gleann Da Eig and head across peat and heather to reach a small dam in the main burn at 60126 42536. The tributary can also be crossed higher up at 60759 43218, from where a wet, high-level path traverses the hillside. From the dam climb up across wet ground to the col at 59731 41994, which leads easily back to the road.

North ridge of Meall Corranaich

GLEN LEDNOCK

ROUTE 59
Ben Chonzie (931m)

Pronunciation: *Ben Chonzie (often pronounced Ben y Hone)*
Translation: *Mossy Mountain*

Distance:	13km
Ascent:	720m
Time:	4hrs
Maps:	OS sheet 51 or 52; Explorer map 368; Area Map 5
Parking:	roadside by footpath sign to Ardtalnaig
Start:	from Coishavachan follow the footpath (which is actually a fairly substantial track)
Hostel:	YHA Killin
B&B/hotel:	Comrie
Camping:	Comrie
Access:	Invergeldie Estate, tel: 01764 670959

Starting from Glen Lednoch, Ben Chonzie offers a fairly simple but pleasant ascent without any real difficulties.

Follow the signposted track, which bypasses the farm buildings at Coishavachan before crossing the Invergeldie Burn. A little higher up the track recrosses the burn just below a small dam. Continue along the track, ignoring a turning to the left which goes to Ardtalnaig by Loch Tay. Near the top of the track, head northeast across grass and heather to reach a line of fence posts on the crest of the broad southeast ridge. Follow these posts to the northwest, then, after a couple of changes of direction, to the northeast. They lead all the way to the summit, which is at the east end of the long flat ridge. A line of shooting

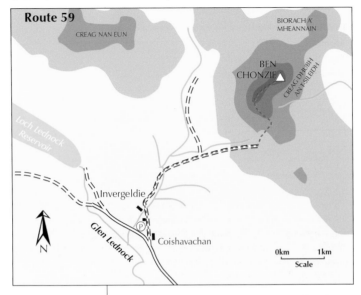

Route 59

CREAG NAN EUN

BIORACH A' MHEANNAIN

BEN CHONZIE

CREAG DHUBH AN T-SIEIDH

Loch Lednock Reservoir

Invergeldie

Glen Lednock

Coishavachan

N

0km   1km
Scale

butts runs along the length of this summit ridge. There is a small cairn and a substantial stone enclosure at the top of **Ben Chonzie** at 77332 30847 (2hrs 30mins).

Return by the same route. The hill can also be climbed from the east via Glen Turret.

CRIANLARICH

ROUTE 60

Beinn Chabhair (933m)

Pronunciation: *Bine Chavair*
Translation: *Hawk or Antler Mountain*

A few hundred metres north of the Stagger Inn, a wooden bridge crosses the River Falloch. The private road on the

Distance:	12km
Ascent:	930m
Time:	4hrs 20mins
Maps:	OS sheet 50; Harvey's Superwalker map Crianlarich; Area Map 5
Parking:	by hotel on A82 in Inverarnan
Start:	along road to footbridge over River Falloch
Hostel:	YHA Crianlarich
B&B/hotel:	Inverarnan
Camping:	Ardlui; Inverarnan
Access:	Glenfalloch, tel: 01301 704229

This rugged little peak stands on the edge of the Crianlarich group. It offers excellent views in all directions, but particularly over the Arrochar Alps and down Loch Lomond. It can be tackled from An Caisteal but is usually climbed on its own from the southern end of Glen Falloch, starting at Inverarnan. A sign requests that dogs are not taken on this walk.

Beinn Chabhair from Beinn a' Chroin

221

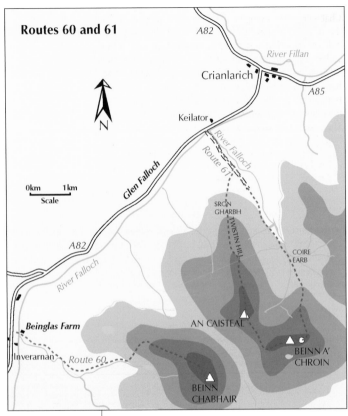

other side of the bridge leads up to Beinglas Farm, but the footpath to the hill does a detour around the farm, first following the line of the River Falloch, then its tributary, the Ben Glas Burn. Cross over the West Highland Way, which passes behind the farm, then climb steeply up the hillside to the east, crossing a stile and following the north bank of the burn, which boasts some pretty little waterfalls along the way. When the angle eases the path becomes quite wet and boggy. Follow it up to the Lochan Beinn Chabhair. From here it veers northeast onto **Beinn**

Chabhair's long, complex, knobbly west ridge. To reach the ridge climb towards the head of a little valley, but halfway up follow a path across to the right side of the valley and around a minor top before the crest of the ridge is reached some way further east. Route-finding here in summer is not a problem as the path is fairly clear, but under snow and in poor visibility the complexity of the ridge with its many rises and falls could be confusing. The easiest line winds around and then over successive hillocks without encountering any difficulties. A small cairn on the north top is passed and a short distance later the main summit cairn is reached at 36750 17968 (3hrs).

Return by the outward route.

ROUTE 61

An Caisteal (995m),

Beinn a' Chroin (942m)

Pronunciation: Un Cashtyal; Bine yuh Kroyne
Translation: The Castle; Hill of Danger or Harm

Distance:	14km
Ascent:	1070m
Time:	5hrs 35mins
Maps:	OS sheet 50; Explorer map 364; Harvey's Superwalker map Crianlarich; Area Map 5; see Route 60 for sketch map
Parking:	lay-by on the A82 at 36947 23885
Start:	from lay-by cross the stile and circle around the field to a bridge over the railway
Hostel:	YHA Crianlarich; Independent Tyndrum
B&B/hotel:	Crianlarich
Camping:	Tyndrum; Inverarnan; Ardlui
Access:	Glenfalloch, tel: 01301 704229

To the south of Crianlarich there are several Munros set into a succession of long high ridges. One of the most interesting routes in this area follows the fine ridge over Sron Garbh and Twistin Hill to An Caisteal and Beinn a' Chroin. By returning via the north ridge of Beinn a' Chroin an excellent circuit can be made.

Start at a lay-by in Glen Falloch on the A82 and cross a stile which leads through a wet field to a farm track. Follow the track under the railway bridge and continue on it alongside the beautiful River Falloch until you reach the corner of the trees on the river's east side. From here Sron Gharbh can be climbed direct. It can be quite wet at the bottom of this hill and it is quite steep near the top, but once you are up this section the worst of the day's slog is over. Climb steadily along An Caisteal's north ridge and up Twistin Hill through a small defile towards the top, then across a small ravine and finally over or round a prominent stubby pinnacle which looms over Coire Earb. None of this presents any difficulty. Continue on for a short distance to **An Caisteal**'s summit cairn at 37874 19336 (2hrs 40mins).

Head southwest past another cairn just a few metres on, then descend the south ridge of An Caisteal. Having come up Twistin Hill you'll recognize this ridge as Son of Twistin Hill. Its twists and turns are a bit more athletic and have a bit more attitude than their gentler namesake further north. Descend to the Bealach Buidhe then follow the path to Beinn a' Chroin. This path takes the most improbable line up the steep crags of **Beinn a' Chroin**'s west face, but artfully it weaves a way without real difficulty in and out of the rocks to emerge triumphant at the west end of the long complex summit ridge. Pass the first cairn and continue to Point 38831 18602, where a small cairn marks the highest point of the hill at 942m (3hrs 50mins).

Or does it? On OS maps and all Munro data pre-dating 2000, the highest point is recorded as being 940m – 2m lower – and not here but ¾km further on at

Beinn a' Chroin's east summit. OS 1:50,000 maps do not even mark a top at this central point before 2002. Actually the east summit even *looks* higher from here, but looks can be deceptive. In fact Harvey Maps, using the latest pictographic mapping techniques, established this middle summit as being the highest point on the mountain at 942m and after some debate other mapmakers agreed, which means that all future Munro data will have to be changed accordingly. Those of a nervous disposition, who fear that the surveyors might have just had an off day when they made this decision, can calm their nerves by continuing across a little col to do the east summit as well, just in case.

The complex summit of Beinn a' Chroin

Return can be made by retracing one's steps over An Caisteal or by heading north from the east summit along the ridge that leads into Coire Earb. Stay close to the crest of the ridge and at the bottom turn northwest and cross the River Falloch, then follow the path and track along the length of the river back to the lay-by.

In winter it would be inadvisable in deteriorating conditions to try to locate the route back to An Caisteal from Beinn a' Chroin, as it could be very hard to find the correct point of descent (at 38369 18304), and the consequences of missing the right line could be very unpleasant. In full winter conditions the ascent of Beinn a' Chroin by this route would in any event be a serious undertaking.

Ardent Munroists may cast an eye over the possibility of including Beinn Chabhair in with the above two hills. It is possible to get from An Caisteal down to a saddle and then steeply up the east face of Beinn Chabhair, trending towards the south side of its summit; however, the descent to the saddle is steep, slippery when wet, and can be unpleasant. Moreover the natural fall of the gullies from the col between An Caisteal and Beinn a' Chroin takes you away from the right line, so if it is attempted the descent should be made from quite high up on An Caisteal's south ridge; all in all, this is not to be recommended.

ROUTE 62

Cruach Ardrain (1046m),

Beinn Tulaichean (946m)

Pronunciation: *Krooerch Ardren; Bine Toolerchine*
Translation: *High Stacked Heap; Hill of the
Little Green Eminence*

This is the central pair of Munros in the Crianlarich group, nestling between the bulk of the Ben More/Stob Binnein ridge system to the east and the ridges of An Caisteal and Beinn a' Chroin to the west. The two Munros are usually climbed together to make a good day's outing and they can be approached from either the north or the south. (The main description below is from the north, and is followed by a note on the route from the south.)

Starting from the A82, park opposite a radio mast about 1km south of Crianlarich, close to a little bridge across the railway line. Cross the bridge and continue on the same

Distance:	14km (12km if done from the south)
Ascent:	1340m (1193m from the south)
Time:	5hrs 15mins (4hrs 55mins from the south)
Maps:	OS sheets 51 and 56 (or Harvey's Crianlarich map); Explorer maps 364 and 365; Harvey's Superwalker map Crianlarich; Area Map 5
Parking:	A82 roadside if approaching from north, or car park east of Inverlochlarig if approaching from south
Start:	at bridge across railway line opposite a radio mast, 1km south of Crianlarich
Hostel:	YHA Crianlarich
B&B/hotel:	Crianlarich
Camping:	9km east of Crianlarich on A85 or Inverarnan on A82; Balquhidder if approaching from south
Access:	Inverlochlarig, tel: 01877 384232. Benmore Farm: 01838 400286

line through a small defile marked by an old post. A line of old fence posts appears which leads into the forest. Follow this line. The gap between the trees in which you find yourself (it is too narrow to be classed as a forest 'ride') should be followed all the way to the open hill. After a few metres the path changes direction to the south, and from this point on it runs pretty much dead straight, passing through a number of open areas and crossing a couple of tracks on the way. The occasional fallen tree adds to the interest. An alternative way of finding the right line is to turn right over the bridge, then back left through a substantial forest ride. This brings you to the fence posts, at which point turn right uphill through the trees.

To describe this route through the forest as a path would involve something of a deception. It is a ribbon of mud which sometimes turns into a fast-flowing burn, and after heavy rainfall there are passages of deep bog that are hard to avoid, for the burgeoning spruce trees on either side constantly push one into the worst of it. Winter is the best time for work like this, when the

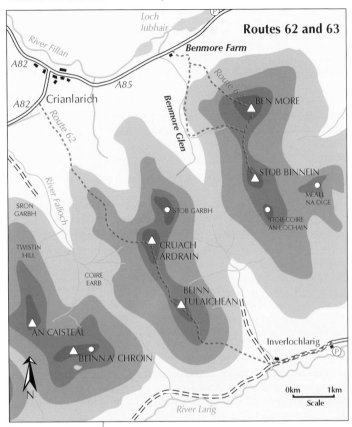

Routes 62 and 63

ground is frozen. After a wet spell in summer it could easily swallow you up. Tread carefully, for you could be treading on the heads of previous parties lost in the mire! Watch out also for aerial attacks from broken branches and swishing pine needles.

Eventually the slough relents and you emerge onto *terra firma* at a distinctive boulder on your left. Continue for a few metres to reach a fence; this is crossed at the highest point of a small bluff just a short distance further on. From here on you can fully enjoy the ridge, heading southeast to reach the Grey Height and from then on staying to the crest of the open, easy-angled ridge which is strewn with a few boulders here and there, some of which are fine perched blocks.

Continue pleasantly to Meall Dhamh, beyond which there is a drop of some 55m before eventually the climb begins to **Cruach Ardrain**. The Munro is not tackled direct. Instead the path skirts around its western flanks before emerging at a col at 40765 20918, a few hundred metres to the southwest of the summit. Head northeast, passing two cairns then descending to a little col before rising again to reach the true summit cairn at 40916 21183 (2hrs 45mins).

To reach **Beinn Tulaichean** retrace your steps across the summit and continue along the ridge, which drops gradually for nearly 1km before rising equally gradually for another kilometre to reach the summit cairn at 41665 19600 (3hrs 30mins).

To return, retrace your steps over the route described.

These two hills can also be tackled from the south starting at Inverlochlarig, once the home and now the

Cruach Ardrain with Stob Binnean behind

Cruach Ardrain with Ben More and Stob Binnean behind, from Beinn a' Chroin

final resting place of Rob Roy. From the car park walk 700m along the private road to the farm at Inverlochlarig and emerge onto the hill by following signs that the farmer has helpfully erected. Once on open ground climb directly to the summit up grassy slopes, which are quite steep at times. An indistinct path becomes more obvious higher up after passing through a gap in a fence. Bracken growing on the lower slopes may be a slight hindrance in the late summer. One or two small outcrops are turned without difficulty until the angle eases and the last few hundred metres run along a broad fairly level ridge to a small cairn which marks the summit (2hrs 20mins).

There are a number of advantages in doing the route from this side. For a start the quagmire through the forest is avoided; secondly there is less vertical ascent and a shorter distance to cover; and finally doing these hills from the south means you have to drive along the beautiful Glen Voil, which is always worth doing.

ROUTE 63

Ben More (1174m),

Stob Binnein (1165m)

Pronunciation: *Ben More; Stob Binnyen*
Translation: *Big Mountain; Anvil Peak*

Distance:	11km
Vertical ascent:	1340m
Time:	5hrs 15mins
Maps:	OS sheet 51; Explorer maps 364 and 365; Harvey's Superwalker map Crianlarich; Area Map 5; see Route 62 for sketch map
Parking:	lay-by on A85, 600m east of Benmore Farm
Start:	a sign indicates the start 100m east of farm
Hostel:	YHA, Killin; Crianlarich
B&B/hotel:	Killin; Crianlarich
Camping:	6km east of Benmore Farm on A85
Access:	Benmore Farm, tel: 01838 400286

The third of the great ridge lines in the Crianlarich group of hills encompasses the huge bulk of Ben More. Ben More is the highest mountain in the group and a dominant feature of this part of the southern Highlands. 'A long steep grind' is a phrase that comes to mind to describe the relentless climb to its top. Actually, some rather more colourful adjectives also come to mind, but they are best left to the imagination.

There is a sign on the main road indicating the start of the path to Ben More, about 100m east of Benmore Farm. Cars often park beside the road here, but it is only ½km further along the road to a lay-by. After a few metres the path joins a farm track that zig-zags up the hillside. Follow the track for a couple of zigs and a zag, passing

This is the sort of route a sadistic sergeant-major would chose to break in his raw recruits. There's nothing for it but to grit your teeth and get on with it. The Forsairean ridge to the northeast of the hill offers a slightly longer but gentler alternative means of ascent; however, the fringe of forest around its base complicates access to that side of the hill. There have been several avalanche accidents on Ben More, dating back to before proper records were kept, and in winter the normal route described here must be regarded as an avalanche black spot.

through a gated fence, then take to the open hillside before the track begins to lose height. There is no clear path at this point and the exact line does not matter much. Essentially the easiest line is up the broad north-west ridge of the hill, staying to the northeast of the steep hanging corrie. Higher up a path becomes clear, which eases the pain. The steep western corrie should be avoided. A 'stane dyke' protects the edge of this corrie, and my undying respect goes to the men who came up

The Crianlarich hills from Sgiath Chuil summit

here to build it. Eventually rocks are reached and the **Ben More** summit cairn appears at 43279 24411. The trig point is a few metres further on (2hrs 50mins).

Head down the south ridge of Ben More, which is fairly broad at first. After a few hundred metres the ridge narrows and is more easily discerned, even in mist. Descend to the Bealach-eadar-dha Bheinn, a fairly wide saddle, before climbing again. The north ridge of **Stob Binnein** is easier going than Ben More, and the eroded path is obvious unless under snow. The summit of this hill is a flattish ridge with the highest point being at the south-west end at 43486 22733 (3hrs 50mins).

Retrace your steps to the bealach. From here the easiest and safest way down is to descend due west to reach the Benmore Burn. A path from the north end of the bealach offers the promise of a shortcut by heading more directly back to the farm, but it disappears after ¾km on fairly steep ground. Once down, continue alongside the Benmore Burn until the farm track is reached at what remains of a wooden bridge. From here it is plain sailing back to the road.

LOCH EARN

ROUTE 64
Ben Vorlich (Callander) (986m),
Stuc a' Chroin (975m)

Pronunciation: *Ben Vorlich; Stook a Chron*
Translation: *Mountain of the Bay; Peak of the Sheepfold*

From the east gate of the Ardvorlich Estate, walk along the track, crossing the burn and passing behind the lodge. The track peters out to become a path. After just over 1km a turning on the left leads into Glen Vorlich and crosses a high pass that eventually leads down into Gleann an

Distance:	13½km
Ascent:	1140m
Time:	4hrs 50mins
Maps:	OS sheets 51 and 57; Explorer map 365; Harvey's Superwalker map Ben Ledi Callander; Area Map 5
Parking:	roadside at Ardvorlich
Start:	through the Ardvorlich Estate's east gate and along private track
Hostel:	YHA Killin
B&B/hotel:	Lochearnhead
Camping:	Strathyre; Balquhidder Station
Access:	Ardvorlich Estate, tel: 01764 685260. The estate requests that walkers don't cross the corrie floor if returning from Stuc a' Chroin across Coire Buidhe, but follow the contours around its edge. If approaching from Glen Ample, contact: 01567 830344.

The upland area between Loch Earn and Callander is where the southern Highlands have their last flourish before the lowlands of the Central Belt are reached. Ben Vorlich and Stuc a' Chroin are the highest points (and also the only Munros) in this area, and their distinctive shapes are visible from many surrounding places.

These hills make a popular excursion from the north, as described here, although they can also be climbed by way of a more lengthy approach from Glen Artney along the Gleann an Dubh Choirein, or from Glen Ample.

Dubh Choirein. Your route keeps to the right-hand path, however, and soon starts the steady climb up the north ridge of **Ben Vorlich**. The way becomes stony near the conical top, but there is never any difficulty finding the right line. The summit trig point is at 62915 18911, and there is a large cairn about 100m to its southeast at a secondary top that is just 1m lower (2hrs 20mins).

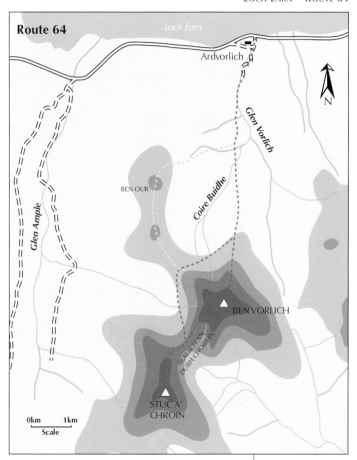

Route 64

Loch Earn

Ardvorlich

Glen Vorlich

BEN OUR

Glen Ample

Coire Buidhe

BEN VORLICH

BEALACH AN
DUBH CHOIREIN

STUC A'
CHROIN

0km   1km
Scale

N

The continuation to Stuc a' Chroin starts off to the west and then follows the main ridge down in a curving line to the wide col below Stuc a' Chroin. Make sure you don't follow a secondary ridge just to the southeast of this one. From the col at the foot of the ridge you now face a steep and imposing rocky prow. Cross some large rust-coloured boulders and climb directly up. The way has

Ben Vorlich from the Bealach an Dubh Choirein

been eroded by the passage of thousands of feet, and there are a number of alternative lines. Those who enjoy looking for difficulty might even prefer to ascend the rocks further to the left. The stiff climb up this nose leads to a cairned top at 61826 17923 and **Stuc a' Chroin** summit lies about ½km further on, where two more cairns are found just a short distance apart. The cairn on the right at 61675 17423 marks the top (3hrs 25mins).

Return to the col below the prow, then drop down to the north side of the corrie, picking up a path that leads to a col on the northwest ridge of Ben Vorlich. From here either skirt around the contours of Coire Buidhe to rejoin the ascent path on the north ridge, or for a little more variety follow the broad northwest ridge over Ben Our and rejoin the path further down.

ARROCHAR

ROUTE 65
Beinn Bhuidhe (948m)

Pronunciation: Bine Vooyuh
Translation: Yellow Peak

Distance:	20km (of which 12km can be cycled)
Ascent:	950m
Time:	6hrs 25mins (4hrs 45mins if using a bike)
Maps:	OS sheet 50; Explorer map 364; Area Map 5
Parking:	car park off the old loop at the northeast end of Loch Fyne
Start:	along private track to northeast of car park
Hostel:	YHA Inveraray
B&B/hotel:	Arrochar; Inveraray
Camping:	A83 south of Inverary; Arrochar
Access:	Ardkinglas Estate, tel: 01499 600261 or 01499 600244

This secretive and complex little hill is well defended with steep sides of crags and wet grass to deter the walker. There is an easy breach, however, at the col just below the northeast top (Point 901). From there a good path weaves around the rocky obstacles along its main ridge giving access to the summit.

From the car park, walk or cycle along the private tarmac road on the east side of the river. (The track that starts to the west of the river joins this road further upstream, but passes through a working gravel pit which can get very muddy and where you are likely to be in the way.) The road can be cycled for 5km or 6km until a sign advises you to leave your bike and walk. A metal frame to which bikes can be locked has helpfully been provided. Continue walking for about 1½km to the derelict cottage at

237

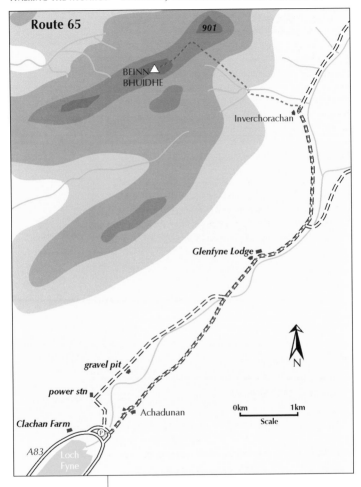

Inverchorachan and just beyond here pass through a gate.
A path leads off to the left here up the south side of a pretty
little burn. Follow this path over a couple of short rocky
sections until you emerge just below a prominent waterfall. Your route lies to the right, but the path continues

climbing to the left of the waterfall onto the upper lumpy moorland where it gradually vanishes (presumably as people realize it is taking them away from their objective). Cross the burn below the waterfall and climb steeply up the grass alongside a small tributary burn. The route from here to the col is rough and pathless; moreover the col does not become clearly visible until you are almost on it because the ground is littered with grassy lumps and rocky knolls that obstruct your vision. Once the ridge is gained, however, it is a pleasant walk for just over 1km to **Beinn Bhuidhe**'s small summit cairn at 20375 18716 (3hrs 45mins; 2hrs 55mins if using a bike).

An alternative ascent can be made by climbing the steep grassy slopes to the north of the burn and passing directly over the rocky crest of the minor top (Point 901). This involves a little easy scrambling.

Return by the route of ascent.

ROUTE 66

Ben Vorlich (Inveruglas) (943m)

Pronunciation: Ben Vorlich
Translation: Mountain of the Bay

Distance:	14km
Ascent:	940m
Time:	4hrs 20mins
Maps:	OS sheet 56; Explorer map 364; Harvey's Superwalker map Arrochar Alps; Area Map 5
Parking:	car park in visitor centre opposite power station in Inveruglas
Start:	along private road to Loch Sloy that starts at 31825 09248
Hostel:	YHA Crianlarich; Inveraray
B&B/hotel:	Ardlui; Tarbet
Camping:	Ardlui
Access:	Inveruglas, tel: 01301 704210

Ben Vorlich, like its neighbour Ben Vane, is a steep-sided mountain, though rather more complex in structure. The northeast ridge is often climbed from Ardlui, as too is the parallel undulating ridge to its east that crosses Stuc na Nughinn and Little Hills. Perhaps the most straightforward (albeit the steepest) approach is from Inveruglas, as described here.

The long south-southeast ridge can be climbed starting from the private road to Loch Sloy; however, it is a very steep ascent to get onto it. Alternatively, by continuing along the road towards Loch Sloy, there are two steep grassy slopes that lead directly onto this ridge just south

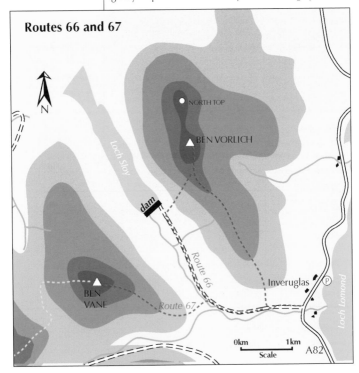

Routes 66 and 67

N

NORTH TOP

BEN VORLICH

Loch Sloy

dam

Route 66

BEN VANE

Route 67

Inveruglas

P

Loch Lomond

0km   1km
Scale

A82

*Loch Sloy dam
and Ben Vorlich
from Ben Vane*

of the summit. Either of these can be climbed – or, for a little variety, the first can be climbed part way and a route can then be negotiated between the crags to the second grassy slope, which rises directly and relentlessly up from the corner of the loch. Pause for breath at the top, then follow the path for about 1km, passing by the first top, to **Ben Vorlich**'s summit cairn at 29498 12457 (2hrs 50mins).

Return by the route of ascent.

Some old Scots pine tree stumps in the peat near Loch Sloy have been radio-carbon dated and found to be over 4000 years old. There are many similar tree stumps in peat bogs across Scotland that have been found to be of a similar age.

Loch Sloy was the first of Scotland's extensive programme of hydro-electric schemes. Twenty-one men lost their lives in tunnelling work during its construction.

ROUTE 67

Ben Vane (915m)

Pronunciation: *Ben Vane*
(from 'Mheadhoin' pronounced 'veeyann')
Translation: *Middle Mountain*

Distance:	11km
Ascent:	920m
Time:	4hrs 20mins
Maps:	OS sheet 56; Explorer map 364; Harvey's Superwalker map Arrochar Alps; Area Map 5; see Route 66 for sketch map
Parking:	car park at visitor centre opposite power station
Start:	walk back along main road, then along private road to Loch Sloy that starts at 31825 09248
Hostel:	YHA Crianlarich; Inveraray
B&B/hotel:	Tarbet; Ardlui
Camping:	Ardlui; Arrochar
Access:	Inveruglas, tel: 01301 704210

At the south end of Loch Sloy this steep-sided little hill comes dramatically into view as you walk along the private road from Inveruglas. Ben Vane sits close beside Beinn Ime and is often climbed in combination with it and Beinn Narnain. It is worth pointing out, though, that a lot of height has to be lost when climbing these three hills together, and on hot summer days many parties underestimate the demands of climbing nearly 1800m of vertical ascent.

From the car park, walk back past the power station to the start of the private gated road to Loch Sloy. Go along this road for 2km, passing a turning on your left to Coiregrogain Farm, and take the next turning ½km further on. This track crosses a bridge and leads round the nose of the southeast ridge of Ben Vane. A smaller second bridge is reached after another ½km at 29542 09235. At

this point leave the track and climb steeply onto the ridge. Continue to climb, steeply at times, through lots of little rocky outcrops all the way to the top. The way is clear and no scrambling is involved. As you pull over the last steep section **Ben Vane**'s summit cairn appears directly in front of you. Surprisingly, after such a stiff climb on an apparently conical hill, the summit is almost flat enough to play football on (though having to retrieve the ball when it went out of play could be something of an irritation). There are good views of the Arrochar Alps, the Ben Lui group and even a good distant profile of Ben Nevis from the top at 27790 09824 (2hrs 45mins).

Return by the route of ascent.

Beinn Ime from Ben Vane

243

ROUTE 68

Beinn Narnain (926m), Beinn Ime (1011m)

Pronunciation: *Bine Narneen; Bine Immer*
Translation: *(possibly)*
Mountain of the Notches; Butter Mountain

Distance:	12½km
Ascent:	1310m
Time:	5hrs 40mins
Maps:	OS sheet 56; Explorer map 364; Harvey's Superwalker map Arrochar Alps; Area Map 5
Parking:	car park by A83
Start:	signposted footpath from north side of A83
Hostel:	YHA Inveraray
B&B/hotel:	Arrochar
Camping:	Arrochar
Access:	Glencroe Farm (for Ben Ime), tel: 01301 702523, dogs on leads. Forest Enterprise (for Beinn Narnain), tel: 01877 382383 or 0131 334 0303

The Arrochar Alps are justly popular throughout the year and comprise some fine Munros as well as Scotland's most weirdly shaped mountain: The Cobbler (Ben Arthur), which has played an important part in the development of Scottish rock climbing. Beinn Narnain's rocky form may not attract the eye in quite the same way as its showy neighbour, but this too is a majestic mountain, its rugged upper reaches well concealed as you approach from the southeast.

From the car park by the A83, just south of Succoth, cross the road and follow the signposted path steeply up through a narrow band of trees. After about 1km the concrete blocks along this 'Pipe' path run out and the

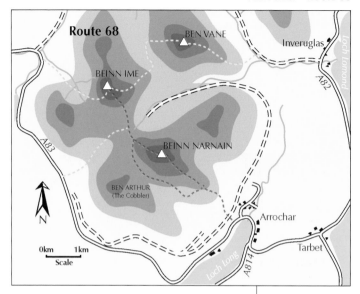

main track, which has been recently upgraded, leads southwest to The Cobbler. To climb Beinn Narnain, however, continue northwest quite steeply up the broad nose of its southeast ridge. Climb a band of wet rocks (which can be icy and tricky in winter). A second band of rocks higher up is split by an easy gully which is climbed

Beinn Narnain from Beinn Ime

245

Beinn Narnain summit rocks from southeast approach

Looking south from Beinn Ime

to easier ground. There is a slight drop before Beinn Narnain's impressive upper ramparts are reached. A path leads round to the left of the main rocks, then picks a route through them to the top. There is a cairn on top of the big rock buttress to your left as you arrive on top, but the trig point and **Beinn Narnain**'s main summit cairn lie a little further on at 27171 06650 (2hrs 30mins).

Continue across the stony summit and exit to the west, where a path drops down to the Bealach a' Mhaim. In poor visibility do not attempt to head directly to Beinn Ime as this would take you over Beinn Narnain's steep northwest face. From the bealach join a path that crosses a fence and climbs the long, grassy southern slopes of **Beinn Ime**. The summit is a rocky outcrop with fine views, topped by a stone enclosure at 25512 08476 (3hrs 50mins).

To return, retrace your steps to the stile over the fence, then continue to skirt around the northwestern slopes of Beinn Narnain to the col between it and The Cobbler. Follow the northeast bank of the Allt a' Bhalachain down past the Narnain Boulders to a small dam. From here either continue straight down and return along the road, or take the path that branches off to the northeast – this brings you back to the top of the Pipe path.

Beinn Ime can also be climbed from Butterbridge to its west, but this is a fairly steep and relentless slog.

LOMOND

ROUTE 69
Ben Lomond (974m)

Pronunciation: Ben Lomond (Gaelic: Beinn Laomainn)
Translation: Beacon Hill

Distance:	11km
Ascent:	1010m
Time:	4hrs 15mins
Maps:	OS sheet 56; Explorer map 364; Harvey's Superwalker map Ben Lomond and Loch Katrine; Area Map 5
Parking:	car park at end of public road to the south of the mountain
Start:	continue north from car park on private road past Ardess
Hostel:	YHA, Rowardennan
B&B/hotel:	Drymen
Camping:	Milarrochy B837
Access:	National Park, tel: 01360 870224. The road in is sometimes closed at times of very heavy use.

This fine, shapely hill is seen to best advantage from the west side of Loch Lomond. It is a huge attraction to hillwalkers and tourists alike and the views from the top, particularly of the Arrochar Alps, do not disappoint.

The best line of ascent is up the Ptarmigan ridge. To reach it follow the private road, passing the youth hostel on the left and another turning on the right. Immediately past the main cluster of houses the road crosses a small burn; the path onto the hill starts here and follows this burn for a short distance before veering north. Stay mostly on the left of the ridge until it levels out. The path then switch-backs over some hillocks before dropping a short way to

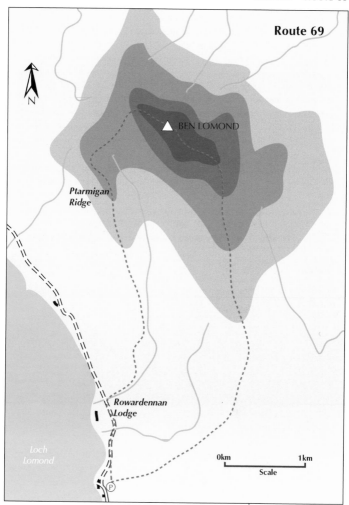

Route 69

Ben Lomond

Ptarmigan Ridge

Rowardennan Lodge

Loch Lomond

0km   1km
Scale

a muddy valley, which is crossed on stepping-stones to reach the foot of the final ridge. This is climbed quite steeply at first to reach **Ben Lomond**'s summit at 36703

249

Its position just a short drive from Glasgow ensures that Ben Lomond, which is the most southerly of all the Munros, is also one of the most frequently climbed. Don't expect to have it to yourself unless you're intent on a mid-week, early-morning, winter ascent. And even then there may be others around with the same idea. Despite recent alterations to the car park it is still not big enough for all the summer traffic at peak times, and the road sometimes has to be closed to prevent gridlock. If you must climb Ben Lomond on a sunny summer weekend, it would be wise to arrive early.

02849 (2hrs 45mins). There are good views from here over the Arrochar Alps and the southern Highlands.

Many people will prefer to return by the same route; the alternative is to follow the main path to the southeast, then south, until it passes through a gate and finally enters woodland, returning directly to the car park.

Ben Lomond from Ben Vane

The Arochar Alps from Ben Lomond's Ptarmigan ridge

APPENDIX 1
Bibliography

Barton, B. and Wright, B., *A Chance in a Million? Scottish Avalanches* (Scottish Mountaineering Trust, 2000)

Bennet, D.J. (ed), *Munro's Tables* (Scottish Mountaineering Trust, 1997)

British Geological Survey (various authors), *British Regional Geology Series*, 'Volume 2: the Northern Highlands', 'Volume 3: The Tertiary Volcanic Districts', 'Volume 4: The Grampian Highlands' (HMSO, London)

Brown, H., *Hamish's Mountain Walk* (Baton Wicks, 1996)

Daiches, D., *Bonnie Prince Charlie* (Penguin Books, 2002)

Dalley, S. and Dalley, J. (ed), *The Independent Hostel Guide* (The Backpackers Press, 2002)

Darling, F. and Boyd, M., *The Highlands and Islands* (Collins, Fontana New Naturalist Series, 1964)

Dixon, C. and Dixon, J., *Plants and People in Ancient Scotland* (Tempus, 2000)

Drummond, P., *Scottish Hill and Mountain Names* (Edinburgh, Scottish Mountaineering Trust, 1991)

Lusby, P. and Wright, J., *Scottish Wild Plants* (Mercat Press, 1997)

Mackenzie, W.C., *Scottish Place Names*, Kegan Paul (Trench and Trubner, London, 1931)

Macleod, A. (translation), *The Songs of Duncan Ban Macintyre* (Oliver and Boyd for the Scottish Gaelic Texts Society, 1952)

Mitchell, I., *Scotland's Mountains Before the Mountaineers* (Luath Press, 1998)

Moran, M., *The Munros in Winter* (David and Charles, 1986)

Moran, M., *Scotland's Winter Mountains* (David and Charles, 1988)

Murray, W.H., *Scotland's Mountains* (Scottish Mountaineering Trust, 1987)

Nicolaisen, W., *Scottish Place-names, their study and significance* (Batsford, London, 1976)

Ross, D., *Scottish Place Names* (Birlinn, 2001)

Scottish Natural Heritage, *Scottish Outdoor Access Code* (2005)

Watson, W.J., *The History of the Celtic Place-names of Scotland* (Birlinn, 1993 (first published William Blackwood and Sons, Edinburgh, 1926))

APPENDIX 2
Contact Details

Avalanche Warnings Internet: www.sais.gov.uk and posted in all major winter resorts

Backpackers Club c/o P Maguire, 29 Lynton Drive, High Lane, Stockport, Cheshire SK6 8JE

Caledonian MacBrayne (west coast ferries) tel: 01475 650100 or 0990 650000

Forest Enterprise (Scotland) 1 Highlander Way, Inverness Business Park, Inverness IV2 7GB tel: 01463 232045 Internet: www.forestry.gov.uk

Harvey Maps 12–16 Main Street, Doune, Perthshire FK16 6BJ tel: 01786 841202 Internet: www.harveymaps.co.uk

Hillphones Internet: www.hillphones.info

Independent Backpackers Hostels Scotland c/o Pete Thomas, Croft Bunkhouse, Portnalong, Isle of Skye, IV47 8SL tel: 01478 640254 Internet: www.hostel-scotland.co.uk

John Muir Trust 41 Commercial Street, Edinburgh, EH6 6JD Tel: 0131 554 0114

List of Munroists if you wish to have your name added to the 'official' list of Munroists, notification of completion can be made to the Clerk of the List, currently David A. Kirk, Greenhowe Farmhouse, Banchory-Devenish, Aberdeenshire, AB12 5YJ. The Mountaineering Council of Scotland will update you of new contact details if there is a change of Clerks.

Mountaineering Council of Scotland The Old Granary, West Mill Street, Perth, PH1 5QP tel: 01738 638227 Internet: www.mountaineering-scotland.org.uk

National Trust for Scotland Wemyss House, 28 Charlotte Square, Edinburgh EH2 4ET tel: 0131 2439300 Internet: www.nts.org.uk

Ordnance Survey Romsey Road, Southampton SO16 4GU tel: 08456 050505
Internet: www.ordnancesurvey.co.uk or www.ordsvy.gov.uk

Police Stations

Aviemore	tel: 01479 810222
Fort William	tel: 01397 702361
Inverness	tel:01463 715555
Portree and Lochalsh	tel: 01478 612888
Strathclyde	tel: 0141 5322000
Tayside	tel: 01764 662212

Rail enquiries tel: 0845 7484950

Sabhal Mor Ostaig the Gaelic College, Slèite, Isle of Skye 1V44 8RQ tel: 01471
888240 Internet: www.smo.uhi.ac.uk/smo/cg

Scottish Natural Heritage currently 12 Hope Terrace, Edinburgh tel: 0131
4474784 (from June 2006 their head office will be at Westercraigs, Inverness IV3
8PG) Internet: www.snh.org.uk

Scottish Tourist Board tel: 0845 2255121 Internet: www.visitscotland.com

Scottish Youth Hostels Association 7 Glebe Crescent, Stirling, FK8 2JA tel: 01786
891400 Central Reservations Service tel: 08701 55 32 55 Internet:
www.syha.org.uk

Weather forecasts
Met Office Area Forecasts for Outdoor Pursuits (updated daily at 0600 and 1800):

West Highlands	tel: 09068 500 441
East Highlands	tel: 09068 500 442

The Weather Centre Lauriston. 'Walk and Climb' weather forecast updated daily
approx 4.00pm tel: 09063 666070

APPENDIX 3

Index of Munros (alphabetical)

Munro	Volume	Page
A' Bhuidheanach Bheag	**1**	**93**
A' Chailleach (Fannaichs)	2	
A' Chailleach (Monadhliath)	2	
A' Chralaig	2	
A' Ghlas-bheinn	2	
A' Mhaighdean	2	
A' Mharconaich	**1**	**88**
Am Basteir	2	
Am Bodach	**1**	**55**
Am Faochagach	2	
An Caisteal	**1**	**223**
An Coileachan	2	
An Gearanach	**1**	**55**
An Riabhachan	2	
An Sgarsoch	2	
An Socach (Glen Affric)	2	
An Socach (Glen Ey/Glenshee)	**1**	**112**
An Socach (Loch Mullardoch)	2	
An Stuc	**1**	**212**
Angels' Peak, The (Sgor an Lochain Uaine)	2	
Aonach air Chrith	2	
Aonach Beag (Loch Ossian)	**1**	**72**
Aonach Beag (Lochaber)	**1**	**41**
AONACH EAGACH, THE	**1**	**133**
Aonach Meadhoin (Glenshiel)	2	
Aonach Mor	**1**	**41**
BEINN A' BHEITHIR	**1**	**129**
Beinn a' Bhuird	2	
Beinn a' Chaorainn (Glen Derry)	2	
Beinn a' Chaorainn (Laggan)	2	
Beinn a' Chlachair	**1**	**68**
Beinn a' Chlaidheimh	2	
Beinn a' Chleibh	**1**	**184**
Beinn a' Chochuill	**1**	**181**

Note: Appendices 3 and 4 cover volumes 1 and 2, and include all recognised Munros. Appendix 3 also includes ranges (shown in capital letters). Routes and ranges in volume 1 are shown in bold.

APPENDIX 4

Index of Munros (by height)

	Height order	Height (m)	Volume	Page
Ben Nevis	**1**	**1343**	**1**	**37**
Ben Macdui	2	1309	2	
Braeriach	3	1296	2	
Cairn Toul	4	1291	2	
Angels' Peak, The (Sgor an Lochain Uaine)	5	1258	2	
Cairn Gorm	6	1245	2	
Aonach Beag (Lochaber)	**7**	**1234**	**1**	**41**
Aonach Mor	**8**	**1221**	**1**	**41**
Carn Mor Dearg	**9**	**1220**	**1**	**37**
Ben Lawers	**10**	**1214**	**1**	**212**
Beinn a' Bhuird	11	1197	2	
Carn Eighe	12	1183	2	
Beinn Mheadhoin	13	1182	2	
Mam Sodhail	14	1181	2	
Stob Choire Claurigh	**15**	**1177**	**1**	**44**
Ben More (Crianlarich)	**16**	**1174**	**1**	**231**
Ben Avon (Leabaidh an Daimh Bhuidhe)	17	1171	2	
Stob Binnein	**18**	**1165**	**1**	**231**
Beinn Bhrotain	19	1157	2	
Derry Cairngorm	20	1155	2	
Cac Carn Beag (Lochnagar)	**21**	**1155**	**1**	**114**
Sgurr nan Ceathreamhnan	22	1151	2	
Bidean nam Bian	**23**	**1150**	**1**	**136**
Sgurr na Lapaich	24	1150	2	
Ben Alder	**25**	**1148**	**1**	**79**
Geal Charn (opposite Ben Alder)	**26**	**1132**	**1**	**84**
Binnein Mor	**27**	**1130**	**1**	**59**
Ben Lui	**28**	**1130**	**1**	**184**
Creag Meagaidh	29	1130	2	
An Riabhachan	30	1129	2	
Carn nan Gobhar	**31**	**1129**	**1**	**100**
Ben Cruachan	**32**	**1126**	**1**	**179**
A' Chralaig	33	1120	2	
An Stuc	**34**	**1118**	**1**	**212**
Meall Garbh (Lawers)	**35**	**1118**	**1**	**212**
Sgor Gaoith	36	1118	2	
Aonach Beag (Loch Ossian)	**37**	**1116**	**1**	**72**

	Height order	Height (m)	Volume	Page
Stob Coire an Laoigh	**38**	**1116**	**1**	**44**
Stob Coire Easain	**39**	**1115**	**1**	**62**
Monadh Mor	40	1113	2	
Tom a' Choinich	41	1112	2	
Carn a' Choire Bhaidheach	**42**	**1110**	**1**	**114**
Sgurr Mor (Fannaichs)	43	1110	2	
Sgurr nan Conbhairean	44	1109	2	
Meall a' Bhuiridh	**45**	**1108**	**1**	**162**
Stob a' Choire Mheadhoin	**46**	**1105**	**1**	**62**
Beinn Ghlas (Lawers)	**47**	**1103**	**1**	**212**
Beinn Eibhinn	**48**	**1102**	**1**	**72**
Mullach Fraoch-choire	49	1102	2	
Creise	**50**	**1100**	**1**	**162**
Sgurr a' Mhaim	**51**	**1099**	**1**	**51**
Sgurr Choinnich Mor	**52**	**1094**	**1**	**49**
Sgurr nan Clach Geala	53	1093	2	
Bynack More	54	1090	2	
Stob Ghabhar	**55**	**1090**	**1**	**166**
Beinn a' Chlachair	**56**	**1087**	**1**	**68**
Beinn Dearg (Inverlael)	57	1084	2	
Schiehallion	**58**	**1083**	**1**	**195**
Sgurr a' Choire Ghlais	59	1083	2	
Beinn a' Chaorainn (Glen Derry)	60	1082	2	
Beinn a' Chreachain	**61**	**1081**	**1**	**170**
Beinn Heasgarnich	**62**	**1078**	**1**	**198**
Ben Starav	**63**	**1078**	**1**	**155**
Beinn Dorain	**64**	**1076**	**1**	**176**
Stob Coire Sgreamhach	**65**	**1072**	**1**	**136**
Braigh Coire Chruinn-bhalgain	**66**	**1070**	**1**	**100**
An Socach (Loch Mullardoch)	67	1069	2	
Meall Corranaich	**68**	**1069**	**1**	**217**
Glas Maol (Glenshee)	**69**	**1068**	**1**	**106**
Sgurr Fhuaran	70	1067	2	
Cairn of Claise	**71**	**1064**	**1**	**106**
Bidein a' Ghlas Thuill	72	1062	2	
Sgurr Fiona	73	1060	2	
Na Gruagaichean	**74**	**1055**	**1**	**55**
Spidean a' Choire Leith	75	1055	2	
Stob Poite Coire Ardair	76	1053	2	
Toll Creagach	77	1053	2	
Sgurr a' Chaorachain	78	1053	2	
Beinn a' Chaorainn (Laggan)	79	1052	2	

	Height order	Height (m)	Volume	Page
Glas Tulaichean	80	1051	1	103
Geal Charn (Ardverike)	81	1049	1	68
Sgurr Fhuar-thuill	82	1049	2	
Carn an t-Sagairt Mor	83	1047	1	114
Creag Mhor	84	1047	1	198
Glas Leathad Mor	85	1046	2	
Chno Dearg	86	1046	1	66
Cruach Ardrain	87	1046	1	226
Beinn Iutharn Mhor	88	1045	2	
Meall nan Tarmachan	89	1044	1	209
Stob Coir'an Albannaich	90	1044	1	159
Carn Mairg	91	1042	1	192
Sgurr na Ciche	92	1040	2	
Meall Ghaordaidh	93	1039	1	206
Beinn Achaladair	94	1038	1	170
Carn a' Mhaim	95	1037	2	
Sgurr a' Bhealaich Dheirg	96	1036	2	
Gleouraich	97	1035	2	
Carn Dearg (Ben Alder)	98	1034	1	84
Am Bodach	99	1032	1	55
Beinn Fhada (Ben Attow)	100	1032	2	
Ben Oss	101	1029	1	184
Carn an Righ	102	1029	1	103
Carn Gorm (Glen Lyon)	103	1029	1	192
Sgurr a' Mhaoraich	104	1027	2	
Sgurr na Ciste Duibhe (Five Sisters)	105	1027	2	
Ben Challum	106	1025	1	201
Sgorr Dhearg	107	1024	1	129
Mullach na Rathain (Liathac)	108	1023	2	
Stob Dearg (Glencoe)	109	1022	1	140
Aonach air Chrith	110	1021	2	
Ladhar Bheinn	111	1020	2	
Beinn Bheoil	112	1019	1	79
Carn an Tuirc	113	1019	1	106
Mullach Clach a' Bhlair	114	1019	2	
Mullach Coire Mhic Fhearchair	115	1019	2	
Garbh Chioch Mhor	116	1013	2	
Cairn Bannoch	117	1012	1	114
Beinn Ime	118	1011	1	244
Beinn Udlamain	119	1011	1	88
Ruadh Stac Mor (Beinn Eighe)	120	1010	2	
Saddle, The	121	1010	2	

	Height order	Height (m)	Volume	Page
Sgurr an Doire Leathain	122	1010	2	
Sgurr Eilde Mor	**123**	**1010**	**1**	**59**
Beinn Dearg (Atholl)	**124**	**1008**	**1**	**95**
Maoile Lunndaidh	125	1007	2	
An Sgarsoch	126	1006	2	
Carn Liath	127	1006	2	
Beinn Fhionnlaidh (Glen Affric)	128	1005	2	
Beinn an Dothaidh	**129**	**1004**	**1**	**176**
Devil's Point, The	130	1004	2	
Sgurr an Lochain	131	1004	2	
Sgurr Mor (Glen Kingie)	132	1003	2	
Sail Chaorainn	133	1002	2	
Sgurr na Carnach	134	1002	2	
Aonach Meadhoin (Glenshiel)	135	1001	2	
Meall Greigh	**136**	**1001**	**1**	**212**
Sgorr Dhonuill	**137**	**1001**	**1**	**129**
Sgurr Breac	138	999	2	
Sgurr Choinnich	139	999	2	
Stob Ban (Mamores)	**140**	**999**	**1**	**51**
Ben More Assynt	141	998	2	
Broad Cairn	**142**	**998**	**1**	**114**
Stob Diamh	**143**	**998**	**1**	**179**
A' Chailleach (Fannaichs)	144	997	2	
Glas Bheinn Mhor	**145**	**997**	**1**	**155**
Spidean Mialach	146	996	2	
An Caisteal	**147**	**995**	**1**	**223**
Carn an Fhidhleir	148	994	2	
Sgor na a' Ulaidh	**149**	**994**	**1**	**150**
Spidean Coire nan Clach	150	993	2	
Sgurr na Ruaidhe	151	993	2	
Sgurr Alasdair	152	992	2	
Carn nan Gobhar (Lapaich)	153	992	2	
Carn nan Gobhar (Strathfarrar)	154	992	2	
Sgairneach Mhor	**155**	**991**	**1**	**88**
Beinn Eunaich	**156**	**989**	**1**	**181**
Sgurr Ban (Fisherfield)	157	989	2	
Conival (Inchnadamph)	158	987	2	
Craig Leacach	**159**	**987**	**1**	**106**
Druim Shionnach	160	987	2	
Gulvain	161	987	2	
Sgurr Mhor (Beinn Alligin)	162	986	2	
Lurg Mhor	163	986	2	

	Height order	Height (m)	Volume	Page
Inaccessible Pinnacle (Sgurr Dearg)	164	986	2	
Ben Vorlich (Callander)	**165**	**986**	**1**	**233**
An Gearanach	**166**	**982**	**1**	**55**
Mullach na Dheiragain	167	982	2	
Maol Chinn-dearg (Glenshiel)	168	981	2	
Meall na Aighean	**169**	**981**	**1**	**192**
Stob Coire a' Chairn	**170**	**981**	**1**	**55**
Slioch	171	980	2	
Beinn a' Chochuill	**172**	**980**	**1**	**181**
Cona' Mheall (Inverlael)	173	980	2	
Ciste Dhubh	174	979	2	
Stob Coire Sgriodain	**175**	**979**	**1**	**66**
Beinn Dubhchraig	**176**	**978**	**1**	**184**
Meall nan Ceapraichean	177	977	2	
Stob Ban (Grey Corries)	**178**	**977**	**1**	**44**
A' Mharconaich	**179**	**975**	**1**	**88**
Carn a Gheoidh	**180**	**975**	**1**	**110**
Carn Liath	**181**	**975**	**1**	**100**
Stuc a' Chroin	**182**	**975**	**1**	**233**
Beinn Sgritheall	183	974	2	
Ben Lomond	**184**	**974**	**1**	**248**
Sgurr a' Ghreadaidh	185	973	2	
Meall Garbh (Glen Lyon)	**186**	**968**	**1**	**192**
A' Mhaighdean	187	967	2	
Sgorr nam Fiannaidh	**188**	**967**	**1**	**133**
Ben More (Mull)	**189**	**966**	**1**	**125**
Sgurr na Banachdich	190	965	2	
Sgurr nan Gillean	191	964	2	
Carn a' Chlamain	**192**	**963**	**1**	**98**
Sgurr Thuilm	193	963	2	
Meall nan Con	194	961	2	
Sgorr Ruadh	195	962	2	
Stuchd an Lochain	**196**	**960**	**1**	**190**
Beinn Fhionnlaidh	**197**	**959**	**1**	**153**
Meall Glas	**198**	**959**	**1**	**204**
Bruach na Frithe	199	958	2	
Stob Dubh (Glencoe)	**200**	**958**	**1**	**145**
Tolmount	**201**	**958**	**1**	**106**
Beinn nan Aighenan	**202**	**957**	**1**	**155**
Carn Ghluasaid	203	957	2	
Tom Buidhe	**204**	**957**	**1**	**106**
Saileag	205	956	2	

	Height order	Height (m)	Volume	Page
Sgurr nan Coireachan (Glenfinnan)	206	956	2	
Stob na Broige	**207**	**956**	**1**	**140**
Sgor Gaibhre	**208**	**955**	**1**	**77**
Beinn Liath Mhor Fannaich	209	954	2	
Am Faochagach	210	954	2	
Beinn Mhanach	**211**	**953**	**1**	**174**
Meall Dearg (Glencoe)	**212**	**953**	**1**	**133**
Sgurr nan Coireachan (Glen Dessary)	213	953	2	
Meall Chuaich	**214**	**951**	**1**	**91**
Meall Gorm (Fannaichs)	215	949	2	
Beinn Bhuidhe (Glen Fyne)	**216**	**948**	**1**	**237**
Sgurr Mhic Choinnich	217	948	2	
Creag a' Mhaim	218	947	2	
Driesh	**219**	**947**	**1**	**119**
Beinn Tulaichean	**220**	**946**	**1**	**226**
Carn Bhac	221	946	2	
Meall Buidhe (Knoydart)	222	946	2	
Sgurr na Sgine	223	946	2	
Bidein a' Choire Sheasgaich	224	945	2	
Carn Dearg	225	945	2	
Stob a' Choire Odhair	**226**	**945**	**1**	**166**
An Socach (Glen Ey/Glenshee)	**227**	**944**	**1**	**112**
Sgurr Dubh Mor	228	944	2	
Ben Vorlich (Inveruglas)	**229**	**943**	**1**	**239**
Binnein Beag	**230**	**943**	**1**	**59**
Beinn a' Chroin	**231**	**942**	**1**	**223**
Carn Dearg (Loch Ossian)	**232**	**941**	**1**	**77**
Carn na Caim	**233**	**941**	**1**	**93**
Luinne Bheinn	234	939	2	
Mount Keen	**235**	**939**	**1**	**122**
Mullach nan Coirean	**236**	**939**	**1**	**51**
Beinn Sgulaird	**237**	**937**	**1**	**147**
Beinn Tarsuinn	238	937	2	
A' Bhuidheanach Bheag	**239**	**936**	**1**	**93**
Sron a' Choire Ghairbh	240	935	2	
Beinn na Lapp	**241**	**935**	**1**	**76**
Am Basteir	242	934	2	
Meall a' Chrasgaidh	243	934	2	
Beinn Chabhair	**244**	**933**	**1**	**220**
Cairnwell, The	**245**	**933**	**1**	**110**
Fionn Bheinn	246	933	2	
Maol Chean-dearg (Torridon)	247	933	2	

	Height order	Height (m)	Volume	Page
Meall Buidhe (Glen Lyon)	248	932	1	188
Beinn Bhreac	249	931	2	
Ben Chonzie	250	931	1	219
A' Chailleach (Monadhliath)	251	930	2	
Bla Bheinn (or Blaven)	252	928	2	
Mayar	253	928	1	119
Meall nan Eun	254	928	1	159
Moruisg	255	928	2	
Eididh nan Clach Geala	256	928	2	
Ben Hope	257	927	2	
Seana Bhraigh	258	927	2	
Beinn Liath Mhor (Coulin)	259	926	2	
Beinn Narnain	260	926	1	244
Geal Charn (Monadhliath)	261	926	2	
Meall a' Choire Leith	262	926	1	217
Stob Coire Raineach	263	925	1	145
Creag Pitridh	264	924	1	68
Sgurr nan Eag	265	924	2	
An Coileachan	266	923	2	
Sgurr nan Each	267	923	2	
Tom na Gruagaich	268	922	2	
An Socach (Glen Affric)	269	921	2	
Sgiath Chuil	270	921	1	204
Carn Sgulain	271	920	2	
Gairich	272	919	2	
A' Ghlas-bheinn	273	918	2	
Creag nan Damh	274	918	2	
Ruadh Stac Mor	275	918	2	
Sgurr a' Mhadaidh	276	918	2	
Carn Aosda	277	917	1	110
Meall na Teanga	278	917	2	
Geal Charn (Drumochter)	279	917	1	88
Beinn a' Chlaidheimh	280	916	2	
Beinn a' Chleibh	281	916	1	184
Beinn Teallach	282	915	2	
Ben Vane	283	915	1	242
Sgurr nan Ceannaichean	284	915	2	

LISTING OF CICERONE GUIDES

AFRICA
Climbing in the Moroccan Anti-Atlas
Kilimanjaro
Trekking in the Atlas Mountains

THE ALPS (Walking and Trekking)
100 Hut Walks in the Alps
Across the Eastern Alps: E5
Alpine Points of View
Alpine Ski Mountaineering Vol 1 Western Alps
Alpine Ski Mountaineering Vol 2 Eastern Alps
Chamonix to Zermatt
Snowshoeing: Techniques and Routes in the Western Alps
Tour of the Matterhorn
Tour of Mont Blanc
Tour of Monte Rosa
Walking in the Alps (all Alpine areas)

CROATIA AND SLOVENIA
Julian Alps of Slovenia
Walking in Croatia

EASTERN EUROPE
High Tatras
Mountains of Montenegro
Mountains of Romania
Walking in Hungary

FRANCE, BELGIUM AND LUXEMBOURG
Cathar Way
Ecrins National Park
GR5 Trail
GR20 Corsica – The High Level Route
Mont Blanc Walks
RLS (Robert Louis Stevenson) Trail
Rock Climbs Belgium and Luxembourg
Tour of the Oisans: GR54
Tour of the Vanoise
Trekking in the Vosges and Jura
Vanoise Ski Touring
Walking in the Cathar region of south west France
Walking in the Cevennes
Walking in the Dordogne
Walking in the Haute Savoie, Vol 1
Walking in the Haute Savoie, Vol 2
Walking in the Languedoc
Walking in Provence
Walking in the Tarentaise and Beaufortain Alps
Walking on Corsica
Walking the French Gorges
Walks in Volcano Country

GERMANY AND AUSTRIA
Germany's Romantic Road
King Ludwig Way
Klettersteig Scrambles in Northern Limestone Alps
Mountain Walking in Austria
Trekking in the Stubai Alps

Trekking in the Zillertal Alps
Walking in the Bavarian Alps
Walking in the Harz Mountains
Walking in the Salzkammergut
Walking the River Rhine Trail

HIMALAYAS – NEPAL, INDIA, TIBET
Annapurna – A Trekker's Guide
Bhutan – A Trekker's Guide
Everest – A Trekker's Guide
Garhwal & Kumaon – A Trekkers' Guide
Kangchenjunga – A Trekkers' Guide
Langtang, Gosainkund and Helambu: A Trekkers' Guide
Manaslu – A Trekkers' Guide
Mount Kailash Trek

ITALY
Central Apennines of Italy
Gran Paradiso
Italian Rock
Shorter Walks in the Dolomites
Through the Italian Alps: the GTA
Trekking in the Apennines
Treks in the Dolomites
Via Ferratas of the Italian Dolomites Vol 1
Via Ferratas of the Italian Dolomites Vol 2
Walking in the Central Italian Alps
Walking in the Dolomites
Walking in Sicily
Walking in Tuscany

NORTH AMERICA
Grand Canyon and American South West
John Muir Trail
Walking in British Columbia

OTHER MEDITERRANEAN COUNTRIES
Climbs and Treks in the Ala Dag (Turkey)
High Mountains of Crete
Jordan – Walks, Treks, Caves etc.
Mountains of Greece
Treks and Climbs Wadi Rum, Jordan
Walking in Malta
Walking in Western Crete

PYRENEES AND FRANCE / SPAIN
Canyoning in Southern Europe
GR10 Trail: Through the French Pyrenees
Mountains of Andorra
Rock Climbs in the Pyrenees
Pyrenean Haute Route
Pyrenees – World's Mountain Range Guide
Through the Spanish Pyrenees GR11
Walks and Climbs in the Pyrenees
Way of St James – Le Puy to the Pyrenees
Way of St James – Pyrenees-Santiago-Finisterre

SCANDINAVIA
Pilgrim Road to Nidaros (St Olav's Way)
Walking in Norway

SOUTH AMERICA
Aconcagua

SPAIN AND PORTUGAL
Costa Blanca Walks Vol 1
Costa Blanca Walks Vol 2
Mountains of Central Spain
Picos de Europa – Walks and Climbs
Via de la Plata (Seville To Santiago)
Walking in the Algarve
Walking in the Canary Islands 1 West
Walking in the Canary Islands 2 East
Walking in the Cordillera Cantabrica
Walking the GR7 in Andalucia
Walking in Madeira
Walking in Mallorca
Walking in the Sierra Nevada

SWITZERLAND
Alpine Pass Route
Bernese Alps
Central Switzerland – A Walker's Guide
Tour of the Jungfrau Region
Walking in Ticino, Switzerland
Walking in the Valais
Walks in the Engadine, Switzerland

INTERNATIONAL CYCLE GUIDES
Cycle Touring in France
Cycle Touring in Spain
Cycle Touring in Switzerland
Cycling in the French Alps
Cycling the River Loire – The Way of St Martin
Danube Cycle Way
Way of St James – Le Puy to Santiago cyclist's guide

MINI GUIDES
Avalanche!
GPS
Navigation
Pocket First Aid and Wilderness Medicine
Snow

TECHNIQUES AND EDUCATION
Adventure Alternative
Beyond Adventure
Hillwalker's Guide to Mountaineering
Hillwalker's Manual
Map and Compass
Mountain Weather
Outdoor Photography
Rock Climbing
Snow and Ice Techniques
Sport Climbing

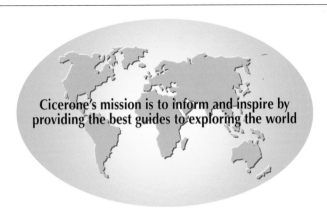

Cicerone's mission is to inform and inspire by providing the best guides to exploring the world

Since its foundation over 30 years ago, Cicerone has specialised in publishing guidebooks and has built a reputation for quality and reliability. It now publishes nearly 300 guides to the major destinations for outdoor enthusiasts, including Europe, UK and the rest of the world.

Written by leading and committed specialists, Cicerone guides are recognised as the most authoritative. They are full of information, maps and illustrations so that the user can plan and complete a successful and safe trip or expedition – be it a long face climb, a walk over Lakeland fells, an alpine traverse, a Himalayan trek or a ramble in the countryside.

With a thorough introduction to assist planning, clear diagrams, maps and colour photographs to illustrate the terrain and route, and accurate and detailed text, Cicerone guides are designed for ease of use and access to the information.

If the facts on the ground change, or there is any aspect of a guide that you think we can improve, we are always delighted to hear from you.

Cicerone Press
2 Police Square Milnthorpe Cumbria LA7 7PY
Tel:01539 562 069   Fax:01539 563 417
e-mail:info@cicerone.co.uk   web:www.cicerone.co.uk